ALSO BY JULIE MORGENSTERN

Making Work Work

Organizing from the Inside Out

Organizing from the Inside Out for Teens

TIME MANAGEMENT
from the
INSIDE OUT

TIME MANAGEMENT
from the
INSIDE OUT

SECOND EDITION

The Foolproof System for
Taking Control of Your Schedule—
And Your Life

JULIE MORGENSTERN

 St. Martin's Griffin 🐃 New York

TIME MANAGEMENT FROM THE INSIDE OUT,
SECOND EDITON. Copyright © 2000, 2004 by Julie
Morgenstern. All rights reserved. Printed in the
United States of America. For information,
address St. Martin's Press, 175 Fifth Avenue,
New York, N.Y. 10010.

www.stmartins.com

Designed by Carla Bolte
Figure art by M&M Design 2000
Illustrations by Janet Pedersen

The Library of Congress has cataloged the
Henry Holt edition as follows:

Morgenstern, Julie.
    Time management from the inside out : the
foolproof system for taking control of your schedule—
and your life / Julie Morgenstern.—2nd ed.
        p. cm.
    Includes bibliographical references and index.
    ISBN 978-0-8050-7590-8
    1. Time management. I. Title.
HD69.T54M66   2004
650.1'1—dc22
                                        2004051807

Originally published by Henry Holt and Company

20 19 18 17 16 15 14 13 12 11

Dedicated to the memory of my father-in-law, Gerardo Colón, whose unconditional love and goodness filled my life and will always inspire me to make time for the people I love

CONTENTS

Introduction   1

PART I: LAYING THE FOUNDATION

1 What's Your Motivation?   9

2 What's Holding You Back?   17

3 Making Time Tangible   37

PART II: QUICK-START PROGRAM

4 The WADE Formula   61

5 Where Paper Meets Time   81

PART III: ANALYZE
Tuning in to Who You Are

6 Choosing the Right Planner for You   103

7 Understanding Your Unique Relationship to Time   125

8 Where Does Your Time Go?   141

PART IV: STRATEGIZE
Designing the Life of Your Dreams

9 Defining Your Goals and Activities   157

10 Time Mapping: Creating Your Ideal Balance   173

PART V: ATTACK
The SPACE Formula

11 Sort   199

12 Purge   211

13 Assign a Home   227

14 Containerize   241

15 Equalize   257

Appendix A: Time Map Worksheet   263

Appendix B: Sources for Time Management
            and Organizing Products   265

Appendix C: Suggested Further Reading   269

Acknowledgments   271

Index   273

TIME
MANAGEMENT
from the
INSIDE OUT

INTRODUCTION

The first edition of *Time Management from the Inside Out* (2000) introduced readers to a new way of looking at time and showed how my foolproof three-step program—Analyze, Strategize, Attack—is as effective for managing time as it is for organizing space. In my role as professional organizer and time management coach, the three-step program has withstood the test of time. I have used it with my clients for almost two decades to help them create the lives of their dreams.

The core of the inside-out approach hasn't changed. Working *with* your personality, instead of *against* it, ensures that the solutions you design will be a natural fit for you, and thus easy to maintain. So what, you're probably asking yourself, is new?

WHAT'S NEW IN THIS EDITION

In the four years since *Time Management from the Inside Out* was released I've traveled the country speaking to a wide range of audiences on this topic. Over the years I've learned that people who attend these talks fall neatly into one of two groups.

The first group consists of people who know they are the masters of their own destiny, but are unsure how to best organize their time or overcome certain obstacles to create the lives they desire.

These people are ready to jump right into talking about their goals and dreams and work on improving their shortcomings.

The second group is hungry for help, too, but these folks come to my seminars feeling like *anything but* masters of their own destiny. Someone else seems to be in charge of their time (i.e., their boss, their company, their kids). When I start discussing big picture goals and dreams, their response is, "You've got to be kidding! I don't have time to think about that. I'm drowning in an endless list of to-dos. I've got to just get out from under!" These people need me to throw them a lifeline. They need practical skills to get them back in charge of their schedules before they can consider diving into the deeper, more reflective aspects of managing their time from the inside out.

So I reorganized and added new material to accommodate those two very different perspectives.

HOW THIS BOOK IS ORGANIZED

This book is divided into five parts, so that you will be able to customize your program and zero in on your trouble spots.

Part 1: "Laying the Foundation." This section helps you define your motivation, diagnose your specific challenges, and master the number-one gateway skill to good time management. A must-read for everyone.

Part 2: "Quick-Start Program." For readers who are drowning under a huge backlog of to-dos and paper (or feel someone else is in charge of their time), this section teaches the basic skills you need to take charge, and provides the breathing room you need to approach the three-step program calmly and with confidence.

Part 3: "Analyze: Tuning in to Who You Are." Here you will create a system that lasts, explore the best planner for your personality, study exactly where your time goes, and understand your unique relationship to time.

Part 4: "Strategize: Designing the Life of Your Dreams." Learn to define your big-picture goals, create activities that will help you achieve those goals, and design a schedule that ensures the balance you desire.

Part 5: "Attack: The SPACE Formula." Put it all together by connecting your daily tasks to your big-picture goals, overcoming psychological obstacles, and maintaining your balance while dealing with the realities of everyday living.

Each of the five parts was designed to be a self-contained unit that has value in and of itself. Yet they are all part of a comprehensive approach designed for lasting change. For most people, the most effective way to work the program is to study one section at a time and then move on to the next. Take your time, and enjoy the process.

TIME MANAGEMENT FROM THE INSIDE OUT FILLS IN THE GAPS

There are many time management books on the market, and most of them contain useful information on prioritizing, avoiding procrastination, and achieving balance. Why is it so hard to follow through on the advice? Because most programs offer tips but gloss over the practical external and internal obstacles to implementation.

For example, they tell you not to overschedule your days, but don't show you how to estimate how long tasks take to complete.

Many stress the importance of creating balance in your life, yet offer no guidance on how to determine what the proper balance would be for you. They warn against the pitfalls of procrastination and chronic lateness, but fail to provide the psychological insight or practical tools you need to overcome these issues. *Time Management from the Inside Out* fills in those gaps so that you can overcome whatever's been holding you back.

Most other time management books also have a particular point of view about what your life should look like. Some suggest you should increase your productivity by 2,000 percent and fill each moment with efficient activity. Others tell you the answer is to let go of the need to be busy and simplify, simplify, simplify.

What these books don't acknowledge is that every reader is different. Some people like a fast pace; others like a slow, easy one. Some people are night owls; others are at their best in the morning. Some people love structure; others thrive on spontaneity and flexibility. And *all* of us have different needs at different points in our lives. The truth is there is no one "right" way to manage your time.

Successful organizing systems work long-term only if they're based around who you are. You can learn new skills and modify some behaviors, but you can't really change your basic personality—and you shouldn't. Your likes, dislikes, needs, and desires must be the foundation of your time-management system. You come first, the system follows, not vice versa.

Time Management from the Inside Out will help you discover who you are, what you want, and what your individual style is. My system offers you a process, not a prescription—so you can design a life that is a natural and comfortable fit for *you*.

WHICH BOOK FIRST?

If you haven't yet read my first book, *Organizing from the Inside Out*, I encourage you to do so. It was designed to be a primer in the process of organizing, and as you regain order in your physical spaces, you will free up an enormous amount of time for yourself. In other words, once you organize your space, you will have much more time on your hands to manage.

However, just as many of my fans have told me that they preferred starting with *Time Management from the Inside Out*. Until they got a grip on their days, they couldn't begin to find time to tackle the clutter in their lives.

My philosophy is this—go with what feels right to you. You basically can't go wrong. If you picked this book up first, it's probably because regaining control over your schedule is the more pressing need.

If you've read *Organizing from the Inside Out* you know that you can use the same Analyze, Strategize, Attack process to organize anything. Yet, I've written a separate book on time management because there are some distinct differences between time and space that make organizing time significantly trickier.

For starters, when you are working with physical clutter, once you have gotten organized, you have much more control over the objects that come into your space than you do over the tasks that invade your schedule. No matter how well you have organized your days or weeks, the outside world constantly imposes new demands and distractions and offers new opportunities. New stuff to sort through just keeps coming.

As a result, a distinction between organizing time and space is the time you'll need to invest in each stage of the process. When organizing a physical space, it only takes about an hour to Analyze and Strategize. The bulk of your time is spent on Attack, taking one to three days per room to dig through the piles of junk. By contrast, when you are organizing your time, the Analyze and Strategize stages take longer because they require more internal reflection than outward observation. You need to spend a few weeks studying yourself to see how you operate in the world before you have the information you need to devise a working plan.

As a result, I've included a brand-new chapter called "Where Does Your Time Go?" to help you conduct that full analysis.

Applying the SPACE Formula to time only takes an instant, but you apply it all day long, every day, day in and day out, until it becomes second nature. In other words, the attack stage never stops. Why? We live in a fast-paced, complex world that presents us with a never-ending flow of options.

Finally, we face a slightly different set of obstacles with time management. When it comes to organizing space, most people assume what's holding them back is a lack of ability (i.e., they just don't know how to organize, or where to begin). They are surprised to discover the role psychology plays in keeping them stuck in their chaos. With time, the opposite is true. When people feel like they are bad time managers, they are quick to blame their own psychology (i.e., they must have a fear of failure or success). However, the more common culprits are technical errors and external factors. By mastering the practical skills of managing your time first, you may find that psychological issues disappear, ostensibly taking care of themselves.

When you use the time-management techniques discussed in this book, you will take control of your days. You'll feel content and happy about how you spend your time. You will maintain a balance between work and love and play that energizes you and makes your life feel rewarding. You will learn how to tune in to yourself, and consistently spend your time in ways that are meaningful to you. *Let's get to it!*

PART I
LAYING THE
FOUNDATION

1

WHAT'S YOUR MOTIVATION?

Do you ever feel like you are off by just a step? That no matter how well you plan your days, or how disciplined you try to be, one unexpected thing comes along and wham . . . you're thrown completely off track?

Does this sound like your life?

The alarm goes off for the fifth time (after half an hour of hitting the snooze button) and the race begins. After speeding through your shower and throwing on some clothes (not the ones you wanted to wear, mind you, because you forgot to pick those up at the dry cleaner), you inhale a quick breakfast, kiss the kids good-bye (after some tense moments at the door about lost backpacks), and dash to the office. The minute you arrive you're hit with one crisis after another. You never have time to look at your to-do list and end up staying late to catch up on tasks that were all due *yesterday*. By the time you finally get home, you're feeling guilty, cranky, and starving. After a patchwork meal of leftovers, you yell at the kids to do their homework and clean up their rooms, then wander the house picking up dirty socks, that morning's newspaper, and a dirty cereal bowl, while thinking about the bills you forgot to pay and the workout that you didn't get to. Eventually, you tumble into bed, exhausted, only to start the race all over the next morning.

> I have so much to do, I don't know where to start. I feel as though my wheels are spinning at one hundred miles an hour and I'm getting nowhere fast.
>
> —*Liz S.*

> I spend more time writing lists than actually getting anything done. I have little notes to myself everywhere, and still I forget things!
>
> —*Susan E.*

> I am good at starting projects but get sidetracked easily. Before I know it, the day is gone and I am left with a million and one unfinished projects.
>
> —*Bill B.*

> Balancing my life is so hard. I'm constantly changing hats between roles: wife, mother, employee, friend, boss. I always feel guilty taking time for myself because there's so much everyone else needs. But, I am soooooo tired at night.
>
> —*Catalina F.*

When life becomes about the million and one things on your to-do list instead of getting to what is most important, and actually enjoying yourself, something is wrong. You don't need to end each day exhausted, depleted, and unfulfilled instead of satisfied. You can get back in balance.

WHAT IS YOUR MOTIVATION?

Why are you reading this book? You picked it up for a reason—because there are meaningful activities you are not getting to. Something essential is missing from your life. What is it? Quality time for your family and friends? Time for a hobby? Time to grow your business? An overall sense of balance?

Before writing this book, I conducted an informal Internet survey and asked my Web site visitors why they wanted to become better time managers. More than 70 percent of fifteen hundred respondents said they wanted to find more time. What varied was what they wanted that extra time for. What do you want?

> I want more time to spend with my friends, to work on craft projects, to have fun.
>
> *—Jenna B.*

> I want more time to talk one-on-one with my kids.
>
> *—Frank R.*

> To gain time for personal enjoyment—reading, listening to music.
>
> *—Lance L.*

> To be able to accomplish things. My bad time management is stopping me from accomplishing my goals in life, especially finishing my Ph.D., so I can be gainfully employed as a psychologist.
>
> *—Paula H.*

> To stop and smell the flowers, instead of trampling over them in a mad rush to be somewhere I should have been an hour ago.
>
> *—Stanley R.*

> I want peace internally—a sense of satisfaction at my accomplishments rather than constant frustration.
>
> *—Becca G.*

> To be able to feel like I can take time to do things I know I need to be doing for *me* everyday (spiritually).
>
> *—Kylie A.*

Right now, at the beginning of this book, write down your own compelling reason. If there were one thing you could add to your life to make you happier and more fulfilled, what would it be? Jot that down on a piece of paper and keep it close by—paper-clip it to your daily planner, pin it to your refrigerator, or place it in your wallet.

I guarantee you that if you follow even one third of the strategies contained in this book, you will be able to add that activity (as well as many other fulfilling activities) back into your life. This one little statement will provide a starting point for your journey to becoming a better time manager, and will help you stay motivated as you learn new skills that may feel awkward at first. It can be a struggle to change ingrained behaviors, but when you focus on what you have to gain, it's easier to succeed.

DEFINING GOOD TIME MANAGEMENT (FROM THE INSIDE OUT)

Time Management from the Inside Out is based on the belief that you have the power to make choices, take ownership, and influence the course of your days—instead of feeling victimized.

Good time management is not about buying a great calendar or planner. It is not about learning tricks to move faster, or about doing everything with mechanical efficiency. It's about creating days that are meaningful and rewarding to you, and feeling a sense of satisfaction in each and every one of your tasks.

Time Management from the Inside Out is about designing a life that is a custom fit for you, based on your unique personality and goals. It's about identifying what's important to you and giving those activities a place in your schedule, and helping you feel deeply satisfied at the end of each day.

There is no "right" way to live your life. I won't tell you to live a simple, calm life, or try to convince you to fill every waking moment with intense, productive activity. This book doesn't contain truisms like "The early bird catches the worm," or impose value systems urging you to either work less or play less, or encourage you to be anything other than exactly who you are. What's offered here is a process, not a prescription.

Time Management from the Inside Out honors and celebrates the fact that you are an individual. It allows for the expression of your unique and personal relationship to time, and the fulfillment of your own personal goals. We each have different needs at different points in our lives. There may be a time in your life when work takes precedence over everything else; another period when family becomes your priority. The tools here allow you to adapt your schedule and days to the changes in your own priorities. The strategies in this book are skills for life.

DEVELOPING A BIG-PICTURE VIEW

No matter how hectic life gets, the most successful people in life have a big-picture view that helps them rise above the chaos and maintain their perspective. A big-picture view is your overriding vision, your belief, simply put, of the meaning of what your life is all about, of what you want it to be. Your big-picture view keeps you on track, providing the context and motivation for all your decisions about how you spend your time.

Your larger view is what keeps you going to the gym, and taking care of yourself, because you understand how feeling healthy and energetic helps you fulfill your other goals. Perspective makes it easier to do tasks you dislike because you understand how each task fits in with your higher life goals.

Your big-picture view gives meaning, motivation, and direction to your life. It's your baseline, your springboard, and your landing place for handling all of life's challenges, choices, and surprises. It becomes easier to cut tasks from your to-do list when you run out of time, while still feeling good about your day. You see that there are many ways to achieve your goal, and no one task will make or break your success.

The program in this book will help you develop your big-picture view and provide you with the practical tools for making your vision a reality. The lessons are presented in sections, starting with new ways of looking at time (part 1), a quick-start program to free up some hours quickly (part 2), and then moving into a full program for designing the life of your dreams (parts 3, 4, and 5). The program in this book follows the natural arc of mastery—focusing on technical skills toward the beginning and addressing psychological factors none fully toward the end.

TOOLS TO GET BACK ON TRACK

What this book will not do is provide a plan that will make your life run perfectly smoothly—no time management system can do that. No matter how well you plan, no matter how organized you are, no matter how skillful you are, there are countless things that could throw a wrench in your day.

Good time managers face that reality. They understand that good time management is not about creating the perfectly balanced life in which everything always goes as expected. It's about having the tools to get back in balance, to come back to center, and to stay true to your own goals when you get thrown offtrack.

The program in this book will help you tune in to who you are and what you want, and then give you the tools to build your life around what's most important to *you*. You can learn new skills and modify some behaviors, but you can't really change your essence—and you shouldn't. Together, we'll go through a process of self-discovery: your likes and dislikes, natural habits, needs, and de-sires. These preferences and little idiosyncrasies will become the foundation of your time-management system and help you recover each time you are thrown offtrack.

So, think back to that one critical task you never seem to find enough time for. Why aren't you getting to that meaningful activity? You may be assuming there just aren't enough hours in the day. But, sometimes, it pays to take a closer look.

The next chapter, "What's Holding You Back," is a diagnostic tool that will help you figure out why you aren't getting to what really counts. Are your issues technical, external, or psychological? You might be surprised by how simple the solutions may be.

2

WHAT'S HOLDING
YOU BACK?

Think about the note you made to yourself at the end of the last chapter, the one important thing you never get to. Is it time for yourself? For your friends? To get your financial house in order? Let's figure out why you are not getting to it. This chapter will help you quickly pinpoint the problem.

A Three-Level Diagnostic

One of the most helpful tools in getting back in balance is knowing what is throwing you off. When people manage their time poorly, they very often jump to the conclusion that they are internally flawed somehow, that they are simply incompetent in this area of life. They may throw their hands up in resignation, convinced that "out of control" is just how life is supposed to be in the modern world. Both of these perceptions are inaccurate and self-defeating.

It's usually a combination of forces that creates time-management problems. Consider the following three levels of errors and obstacles to accurately diagnose what is going wrong. When you understand all the causes of your problem, you can create true change from the inside out.

- **Level 1: Technical Errors.** Perhaps all that is standing between you and what you want to accomplish is an easily resolved mechanical mistake. You may have never learned a particular skill or technique, but once you do you can simply make the appropriate adjustments to your approach and you're all set. Problem solved.
- **Level 2: External Realities.** It would be counterproductive to deny the fact that sometimes environmental factors beyond your control directly interfere with your ability to manage your time and tend to what you consider most important. By identifying the true source of the problem, you can more directly address, adapt to, or manage the issue.
- **Level 3: Psychological Obstacles.** Sometimes, internal forces and fears prevent us from achieving the life we desire. By recognizing certain self-sabotaging habits, you can begin to break free of their control.

Each time you get thrown off track, use the diagnostic below to ask yourself, "Is my problem technical, external, or psychological?" For example, if you are having trouble delegating, the problem could be technical (You don't know how to do it), external (There's no one you can delegate this to), or psychological (You feel guilty asking someone else to do this for you.).

If the problem is multifaceted (as is often the case), I encourage you to tackle the technical errors and external realities first. It's been my experience that once you overcome the problem pragmatically, the psychological resistance usually melts away. This book was organized in such a way that you'll be focusing on practical skills first, then on whatever psychological issues may be holding you back.

Try rereading this chapter whenever you get stuck, and ask yourself what's causing the problem right now. You may discover that there are certain obstacles that tend to cause problems for you over and over again. Ultimately you'll learn to recognize them when they surface, quickly diffuse them, and stop them from sabotaging your efforts to manage your time.

LEVEL 1: TECHNICAL ERRORS

Error #1: Tasks Have No "Home"

One of the most common causes for not getting to important activities is that you haven't set aside a specific time in which to do them. If you think you'll pay bills or write a thank-you note when you are in the mood, think again. When you catch yourself thinking, "I'll have fun, or pamper myself in my spare time," stop! There is no such thing as spare time!

As it is, our days are already packed with more things to do than there will ever be time for. The only free moments we get are when some other activity falls through at the last minute. Unfortunately, because we're caught off guard we usually can't think of what to do with those unexpected moments.

So if something is really important to you, set aside a specific time in your schedule to make it happen. You'll learn more in chapter 4, "The WADE Formula," chapter 10, "Time Mapping: Creating Your Ideal Balance," and chapter 13, "Assign a Home," about how to assign "homes" for each task.

Error #2: You've Set Aside the Wrong Time

If you've set aside time to do something but find yourself still not getting to it, it's possible that you've set aside the wrong time. We all have unique energy and concentration cycles: Some of us are morning people; others are more energetic at night. Other factors can impact our motivation as well: sunshine, the time of year, life circumstances, and how much rest we are operating on.

If you are working against your own natural rhythms, it will be hard to effectively tackle a task when you've planned to. If you can't bring yourself to balance your checkbook each month, maybe the problem is that you're always trying to do it at night after work, when your mental energy is low. If you schedule the task in the morning instead, you might find yourself more motivated to tackle those figures.

For more about working with your natural energy cycles, see chapter 7, "Understanding Your Unique Relationship to Time."

Error #3: You've Miscalculated How Long Tasks Take

Most people are very unrealistic about what they can accomplish in a day. If the time required to complete your to-dos exceeds the time you have available, you simply won't get to it all and will end up feeling frustrated and demoralized. This is completely avoidable. If you get better at calculating how long tasks take, you can plan a realistic workload. Learning how to estimate how long tasks take is a skill anyone can learn, as you will see in chapter 3, "Making Time Tangible." Furthermore, when you know what your big-picture goals are, it will be much easier to eliminate, shorten, or delegate tasks that don't serve your bigger picture. Chapter 4, "The WADE Formula," and chapter 12, "Purge," will help you reduce your workload to fit the time allotted.

Error #4: You're the Wrong Person for the Job

Too many of us make the mistake of thinking that we have to do it all, and that asking for help is a sign of weakness. It can be hard to admit that when it comes to certain tasks, you're simply the wrong person for the job. But it can also be liberating. We each have unique talents and skills, and so do other people. It can save a lot of time, headaches, and heartaches to admit that someone else can do a job faster, better, and more efficiently than you. Maybe you have an assistant, or friends or family members, who would actually enjoy a job that's difficult and tedious for you. If someone else is better at balancing your checkbook or designing a new sales brochure, accept that, hire them, and move on.

You'll learn more about the art of delegating in chapter 4, "The Wade Formula," and chapter 12, "Purge."

Error #5: The Task Is Overly Complex

If you are not getting to what's important to you, it may be that the way you are approaching the task is overcomplicated. A too-large task can be so intimidating that it will cause you to procrastinate.

If you want to see success, you need to simplify the task.

Maybe you've got a dozen boxes full of family memorabilia in your garage, courtesy of your dear departed great-aunt Mimi. Every time you think about them (usually on a sunny Saturday morning), the mere idea of spending the day sorting through a bunch of dusty old boxes is exhausting and you banish the thought from your mind.

However, if you break down the project into smaller steps it becomes more manageable. You could spend just a couple of hours one day taking quick stock of the kinds of things you have to deal with, dividing them into categories that make sense to you (e.g., photos, letters, clothing). On another day you could buy photo boxes and storage containers for other items. Then spend an hour a week organizing photos into albums or separating keepsakes from clothing you'll donate, until you work your way through it all.

Break complex projects into small steps and keep it simple. Chapter 3, "Making Time Tangible," offers tips on breaking down large projects and chapter 14, "Containerize," puts a lid on perfectionism.

Error #6: You Can't Remember What You Have to Do

If you don't have a single reliable to-do list or planner, chances are you won't get to many of your important tasks simply because you won't remember that you have to do them! This sounds overly simplistic, but in the busy, overstimulating environment we live in, it's hard to rely on memory alone. Even with the best intentions, we often get distracted. To avoid this, you will need to consistently record your to-do lists and appointments—including the appointments you make with yourself or your family—in one dependable place. Chapter 6, "Choosing the Right Planner for You," will help you pick a planner that you can live and work with.

Error #7: Your Space Is Disorganized

Even if you are an otherwise excellent time manager, a disorganized physical environment will steal a huge amount of time and energy from your day. You'll waste hours searching for your keys, your reading glasses, or some important document. You'll work inefficiently, get stuck redoing lost work, and have to run out and replace items you can't find.

The solution to this technical error is simple: Organize your space. The average office takes just three days to organize; the average room in a home takes one to one and a half days.

It's too overwhelming to organize everything all at once, but you can start with the room in which you spend the most time. The sooner you invest the time organizing, the sooner you will gain the extraordinary benefits of more time to work with. Read chapter 5 to understand the unique relationship between time and the backlog of papers on your desk. My first book, *Organizing from the Inside Out*, will teach you a simple, foolproof plan for taking control of any space in your home or office.

Error #8: There Is an Absence of Planning Time

Do you get so caught up in being busy and productive that you loathe taking a few minutes out of your life to do any planning? "Measure twice, cut once" is an expression I used to hate, because I never had any patience for planning. I just wanted to jump in and figure things out as I went along. It felt to me like a terribly inactive, nonproductive waste of time, especially when I was under a lot of pressure to get things done. I have since learned that the busier you get, the more essential it is to take a step back, evaluate your priorities, and plan how, exactly, you are going to get things done. Planning prevents you from making mistakes, keeps you focused on what's most essential, and reduces your overall worry factor. It enables you to anticipate obstacles and either avoid them or develop a strategy to minimize their impact. From preparing your daily to-do list, to figuring out shortcuts for cumbersome projects and reviewing your lifetime goals, planning is as productive an activity as checking off anything else on your to-do list. If you invest the time to plan, you will find yourself making the time you need to get to what is most important. Chapter 4, "The WADE Formula," chapter 9, "Defining Your Goals and Activities," chapter 10, "Time Mapping: Creating Your Ideal Balance," and chapter 15, "Equalize," all contain strategies and techniques to plan your work, then work your plan.

Error #9: You Have an Unrealistic Workload

The tricky thing about an unrealistic workload is that it can be attributed to many causes: the technical error of miscalculating how long things take, the psychological drive to work too hard, or external factors—sometimes you just have to admit that life has overloaded you at the moment. Maybe you are working, going to school, and trying to raise children. Maybe your assistant recently moved on, your computer crashed, or your home-renovation project has gone horribly awry and your to-do list is rapidly filling up with tasks you didn't—and couldn't—anticipate.

Regardless of the cause, you can approach work overload as a technical issue. It's time to reexamine your workload and focus on self-preservation. Be kind to yourself. Get rid of extraneous tasks;

streamline and delegate them. Dramatically lower your standards for certain to-dos, just to keep your head above water.

Chapter 4, "The WADE Formula," will help you learn how to reduce your workload, and chapter 12, "Purge," will help you learn to depend on others to get things done. Chapter 15, "Equalize," will help you adapt and adjust your plans and expectations during extenuating circumstances. By following the program in this book, you will be able to create a custom time-management system for yourself that is flexible enough to accommodate the ebbs and flows of a constantly changing workload, as well as unexpected events and crises.

LEVEL 2: EXTERNAL REALITIES

External realities are situations in which you are faced with significant time-management challenges beyond your control. They have a profound impact on your ability to manage your time. When you recognize external realities you can get to the heart of the problem and figure out a way to adapt to them, instead of wasting time and energy beating yourself up. Think about the one thing you'd like to find more time for and see if you recognize your situation in one of the following causes. If so, try a different approach.

External Reality #1: A Health Problem Limits Your Energy

Maybe you aren't getting to what's important because you just don't have the energy reserves to pull it off. Experts say we're a nation of sleep-deprived souls and it's a diagnosis to be taken seriously; lack of sleep can sap you of energy as well as the ability to focus and do difficult analytical tasks. Some people suffer from chronic conditions that seriously deplete their energy stores. You could be slowed down by clinical depression, or attention deficit disorder, or any of a number of health problems that you may not even be aware of. Lethargy that won't go away could signal a thyroid problem, sleep apnea, or a nutritional deficiency.

If you suspect a health problem, don't add worrying about it to your to-do list. And don't be mad at yourself. Instead, make an appointment to see your doctor and ask about the possibility of an underlying medical condition. Take care of yourself and make adjustments for temporary or permanent health and energy problems. If your energy is limited, it becomes more important than ever to prioritize your to-do list: plan your days to start with what's most important, leaving smaller, less significant acitivites for later in the day (and only if you still have any energy left). Chapter 4, "The WADE Formula," and chapter 12, "Purge," will help you create shortcuts and learn to delegate to get the help you need. Chapter 10, "Time Mapping: Creating Your Ideal Balance," will help you create a schedule that works with your energy levels instead of trying to ignore your limitations.

External Reality #2: You Are in Transition

When you're in transition, it's very hard to figure out how to spend your time. Routines fly out the window as you grapple with new responsibilities, demands, and activities. Transitional situations that can throw your schedule off include getting married, getting divorced, a job change, a new baby, illness, retirement, graduation, and moving.

When you're disoriented by a transition, reground yourself by identifying one or two activities that always anchor you (exercise, sleep, time for loved ones), and make sure you build time for those activities into your schedule. Then build a new framework around those grounding activities that accommodates your new lifestyle, understanding that it may change. Chapter 10, "Time Mapping: Creating Your Ideal Balance," will help you claim time for the most essential activities, even during a time of transition.

External Reality #3: You Are in an Interruption-Rich Environment

The interruption-rich environment is a challenge for even the best time managers. A mom with a newborn can't control when her baby sleeps and wakes; a doctor can't control when his patients will need emergency care. Public relations people, real estate agents, stockbrokers, salespeople, and many others in service-based industries all have interruption-rich jobs that require them to be extremely responsive to others.

How do you handle an interruption-rich environment? By acknowledging and planning for it. Leave plenty of time for the interruptions and crises. Then create a little oasis of time for yourself that is totally under your control by putting your phone on voice mail, or asking a colleague to fill in for you, or waking up a little earlier each day. And make sure you do what's most important to you in that oasis of time.

Chapter 10 will teach you how to develop a Time Map that allows you to create these havens free of interruption, and chapter 12, "Purge," will help you master delegation.

External Reality #4: Other People's Chaos

What if you are living or working with somebody whose disorganized ways keep interfering with your own time-management plans? If there is anyone whose disorganization affects you on a regular basis— a chaotically driven spouse, child, boss, coworker, client, or business partner—you'll need to resolve the conflict in order to eliminate your anger and keep the relationship healthy. If you can, get this person to work with you on improving his or her own time management.

Remember that the best negotiations always start out by identifying the common goals you have with the other person. This will eliminate any defensive feelings and put both of you on the same side of the fence. With a boss, your common goal may be to produce the best widgets in the country. With a spouse, your common goal may be to create a happy home. Then, as a team, you can brainstorm ways to prevent last-minute chaos.

If you can't negotiate a solution, you will have to take responsibility for protecting your own schedule. Stop relying on your friend to go to the gym with you if she always cancels at the last minute. Announce an earlier meeting time for someone who is perpetually late. Be smart and accept other people's quirks, and change your approach in relation to them.

LEVEL 3: PSYCHOLOGICAL OBSTACLES

Sometimes what stands between our current, chaotic lives and the lives in which we make time for what's really important are psychological obstacles. We know what we need to do, but we resist taking action because the inaction serves us somehow by fulfilling some deep-seated need we may not even be aware of. Without awareness, these forces will sabotage your best efforts to make time for what you deem most meaningful.

Often, just realizing what you've been doing and why you might be doing it is enough to move you toward change.

In my years of hands-on practical experience in the organizing field, I've discovered the following common themes among clients who are struggling to get a grip on their time. Does any of the following sound familiar?

Psychological Obstacle #1: Unclear Goals and Priorities

Without clearly defined goals, it's nearly impossible to follow through on your plans or to make decisions on how and where to spend your time. You have no basis for how to prioritize and sift through the many choices that confront you on a daily basis.

Perhaps you've got general goals, but you haven't taken the time to write them down or think them through completely. When they're not clear, trying to reach them is like trying to navigate your way through a strange city with a sketchy map—frustrating and riddled with opportunities to make wrong turns.

GETTING REAL

Pete, Management Consultant

Pete, a management consultant who founded his own firm after fifteen-plus years working for one of the biggest-name consulting companies around, knew that his overall goal was to create a successful business. Pete had always flourished in his career—and knew he wanted his own firm to thrive—but had never actually defined what *thriving* meant *to him*. Did he want his business to be the next Merck, or did he want to make his one-man operation more profitable? He didn't know, and made unfocused decisions that led to costly detours.

When an old colleague offered him a decent deal on office space downtown, Pete grabbed it. Without much thought he figured his own office space would have cachet—and surely a "downtown" address would boost his tiny firm's profile.

It was only after he had committed to an expensive long-term lease that he realized how much he treasured the lifestyle his home-based business offered. After fifteen years wearing a suit and tie, Pete loved that he could work—all day if he wanted to—in his jeans and a T-shirt. He loved being able to work whenever he wanted to—flexibility that gave him more time to spend with his family. Most of all, he liked being able to pick and choose his own clients and projects—he could work with clients he liked best, and on the projects he found most interesting.

Pete eventually figured out that *thriving* for him meant being able to spend more time working on the things he cared about, maintaining a flexible schedule, and making a comfortable-enough living. Do you think he would've made a different decision about the lease had he known that ahead of time?

Maybe you know you want a rewarding family life, but, like Pete, haven't defined specifically what that means to you. Does it mean taking your family on cross-country trips every summer? Or having dinner together every night? If your goals are not well defined, you're probably having a hard time focusing your energies, deciding which opportunities to act on and which to decline.

I am convinced that most people know in their hearts what they want. The problem is that somewhere along the way we lose sight of or deny our desires and dreams. Or, you may say you want something, but actually feel conflicted about it. If you aren't where you want to be, you are either on your way (and good for you), or not so sure you really want to go there. Ask yourself if you are just afraid to articulate what you want. If you have the courage to visualize success, you can make anything happen.

Chapter 9, "Defining Your Goals and Activities," will help you clarify your thinking about your goals and determine what your biggest priorities in life are.

Psychological Obstacle #2: Conquistador of Crisis

Think about the one big thing you never have time to do. Do you thrive so much on being busy, on getting things done, on checking off one accomplishment after the next, that you end up leaving the one thing that's really important to the very last second—and then run out of time? If your life feels like one urgent calamity after another, chances are you are a "conquistador of crisis."

You set your life up to be in constant disaster mode because, quite frankly, you are a wonderful crisis manager. You feel so good conquering the impossible that you keep creating it, just so you can rescue yourself. You pull it off every time—though not necessarily without some "fallout" along the way.

If you are a conquistador of crisis, you may have trained for this role as a kid playing the role of the group organizer, peacemaker, or problem solver. You learned to feel a certain comfort in crisis, and you felt good about your ability to handle chaos. The ability to act swiftly and successfully in crisis is a wonderful quality! Just make sure that the mayhem you keep creating (for the purposes of taming) is meaningful to you—don't fritter away these skills on to-dos and activities that aren't important to your bigger picture. You can learn to feel good about your "conquistador" abilities, without having to test it on a daily basis. Chapter 9, "Defining Your Goals and Activities," will help you focus on the things most important to you, and chapter 12, "Purge," will help you scrap the things that aren't.

Psychological Obstacle #3: Fear of Failure or Success

If you know what your goals are, but are not getting to the things that are important to you, it could be that you are suffering from a fear of failure. It can be very frightening to go after your dreams and find out you are incapable of achieving them. Sometimes it's easier to avoid making the effort, blaming circumstances or the fact that you didn't get to try, rather than risking true failure. Even the thought of failure can seem devastating to some people. Think about the tasks or activities that you've been avoiding because you're afraid of messing them up. How about really taking control of your finances? It's scary! What if you make a mistake? Or discover that the plan you've been mulling over in your mind is unattainable? Being unwilling to risk failure will prevent you from attaining your goals, because you're forever afraid to take that first step. When failure has you paralyzed in its grasp ask, "What's the worst possible thing that could happen?" and then dare yourself to move forward.

On the other hand, success can produce just as much anxiety as failure can. You might not be pursuing your goals because you fear the reactions of the people around you—your boss may not like it, your kids may balk, your spouse may act confused—because they're used to things the way they are. If you are afraid to disrupt the status quo, you may be forsaking what's most important to you for what is comfortable, safe, or secure.

Once you recognize this fear of success, it's much easier to move through it. Everyone deserves success. If you harbor this fear, spend time with people you consider successful. It will demystify the scary aspects and make success feel within your reach.

When you are fearful of change, remember that you may be able to make the change in such a way that it's more gradual and less wrenching. Taking small steps will give you and others a chance to adjust. Chapter 9, "Defining Your Goals and Activities," will help you figure out what your goals are, and then help you determine manageable ways to achieve them.

Psychological Obstacle #4: Fear of Downtime

For some people, "downtime" is very anxiety provoking. If this is you, the idea of taking a day off with nothing to do, taking any time for yourself, or simply slowing down enough to relax consumes you with dread.

Maybe you feel guilty taking time off because you're not as productive. Or maybe you take a certain pride in being constantly on the go or completely consumed by one project after another.

All work and no play may not make you dull, but it is a recipe for burnout.

You may actually be keeping your schedule packed and your mind cluttered to avoid thinking about larger, more difficult issues, like what you really want to do with your life, or how to deal with an unhappy marriage, or a big decision. With a calmer schedule and time to think, you may have to begin dealing with matters you've consciously or unconsciously been ducking.

You don't have to stop being busy—you can keep a packed schedule if that's how you're most comfortable. But make sure that you fill your time with a set of balanced activities that are meaningful to you, instead of busywork.

Psychological Obstacle #5: Need to Be a Caretaker

Sometimes, we get so caught up in our own need to be appreciated and feel valued that we don't allow other people to help us. Feeling a sense of pride in being able to accommodate anyone who asks a favor of you is understandable—we all like to be needed; that sense can give us value, meaning, and definition.

But you can't say yes to everyone—there simply isn't enough time in the day. When your caretaker impulse goes into overdrive, it can cause you to feel resentful, underappreciated, and drained: You keep saying "yes," but no one ever seems satisfied with the time you give them; everyone wants more, more, more! Consider this: Saying yes to the person in the moment means you're saying no to someone else whom you've already promised that time to. If you're always staying late to help out a coworker, or say "sure" to every committee assignment that's offered to you, whom or what are you saying no to? Is it your spouse? Your kids? Your friends? The gym? Alone time? Leashing your caretaker role will ensure that you are actually taking care of the people who are most important to you (and yourself!), instead of giving priority to anyone who catches you in a generous moment.

GETTING REAL

The Caretaker

Sara, thirty-five and single, is a highly accomplished professional who's never led a balanced life. Warm, giving, and dynamic, she's notorious among friends and family for canceling plans at the last minute because of work conflicts.

To me she confessed, "I give the appearance of having an incredibly demanding job, but the truth is I often use work as an excuse for getting out of social engagements." Why? Because in every relationship, she took on the role of caretaker, therapist, friend, boss, or mother. It was exhausting, yet she couldn't imagine going into a social situation focused on anything other than how she could help people—it was her identity.

About two weeks into our work together the fates conspired to land her in the hospital where she had no choice but to allow family and friends—and there were plenty of them—to help. It felt strange, but in a good way. Long talks with her father and sister opened her eyes to the fact that her fierce independence, and insistence on not needing anyone's help, often felt like a rejection. Sara had never even considered that possibility—she simply didn't want to burden other people.

Over the next several weeks, as she recovered from her illness and slowly returned to the rhythm of normal life, Sara started to delegate more work to her staff. She made dinner plans with friends and kept them. She signed up for Pilates classes and didn't miss a session. With time, she came to see life outside the office as refreshing, not the burden it once was. It seems that in taking care of herself, she got even better at taking care of others.

See chapter 12, "Purge," for advice on how to just say no.

Psychological Obstacle #6: Fear of Completion

Some people have a hard time making progress toward their goals and getting through their to-do lists because they actually have a fear of completion. They keep starting projects, bouncing back and forth between all of them, yet have a hard time finishing any one project. They never get to truly enjoy a feeling of accomplishment, and the result is a loss of energy and self-esteem.

Often people have a hard time finishing projects because they love the creative process and hate having to make choices that will close off other options. If this is the case, keep reminding yourself that there will always be new projects and new chances to flex your creative muscle. It can be helpful to think about your role shifting from creator to editor at a certain point in the project's development. Once the creator has had a fair turn at the project, it's time to let the editor take over. Another technique is to spend time with people who love to get things done, or to team up with someone who's a "finisher" and let them put the project to bed. Sometimes, through osmosis, you can learn to savor the joy of completion.

If you don't finish a project and it keeps lingering on, sometimes it's simply because the project is no longer important to you. Give yourself permission to let go of the time and effort you have invested. When you let go of the obsolete, you free yourself up for new projects. Chapter 14, "Containerize," will offer more advice on seeing things through to completion.

Psychological Obstacle #7: Need for Perfection

Perfectionists feel compelled to do everything at the same level of excellence. Many adopt the attitude, "Well, if I can't do this perfectly, I'm not going to do it at all!"

The need for perfection often comes out of a need for approval.

It could also come from a fear of criticism, humiliation, or harsh judgment. Maybe the perfectionist mantra was drummed into your head as a kid and you never learned how to evaluate which tasks were worth your very best effort and which ones weren't. Or it could be that you feel more secure when everything seems to be under your control.

One client of mine had been intending to "get back to the gym"—but she insisted on finding the *perfect* gym, with the *perfect* classes, and the *perfect* trainer, who would design the *perfect* workout program for her body type. But she'd been talking about this for a year and hadn't made one inch of progress! Others get caught up on bill-paying. They go crazy trying to find the *perfect* software program, and spend hours worrying about having a *perfectly* balanced checkbook and keeping a *perfect* record of their expenditures.

Some things in this world are worth doing perfectly—but lots of times, good enough is good enough. If your perfectionism is preventing you from accomplishing a task or project, find a way to make yourself get started. Instead of finding the *perfect* gym, join a health club recommended by a trusted friend; instead of using a fancy software program, just get yourself set up to pay online. At least then, you'll have something to work with. For help in learning when enough is enough, see chapter 14, "Containerize."

Psychological Obstacle #8:
You Fear Structure Will Stifle Creativity

Many creative or "right-brained" people fear that imposing structure in their lives will squelch their creativity or their free-spirited personality. As a result, their personal and business lives are chaotic and cause them tremendous stress.

If this is your situation, be assured that imposing structure can actually be liberating. Many of the most successful creative writers, artists, and musicians find great freedom in structure and discipline. They write or paint or draw at the same time every day. Some days the creativity flows, others it trickles out, but the consistency of their schedule assures that they make time for what is important to them.

Structure doesn't destroy your creative impulses; rather, it allows them to flourish. After all, when your schedule is free-form, you often don't get to the things that are most important to you. Your creative work takes a backseat to the more urgent demands of other people, and you neglect your own needs, such as paying your bills and making doctors' appointments.

You need to learn to trust that you can put structure into your schedule and still have enough freedom to hear the call of your muse, or respond to opportunities that crop up, or spend time with your friends, customers, and associates. You don't have to plan every hour, but you can map out a general rhythm to your day.

If you are afraid of structure, *Time Management from the Inside Out* will work well for you because it will allow you to accommodate your natural behavior patterns. You can customize your schedule to work for you, as you will see in chapter 10, "Time Mapping: Creating Your Ideal Balance."

Becoming aware of what has been holding you back can make a monumental difference in your effort to gain control over your time. Fortified with these new insights into why you act the way you do, you have a real head start in creating long-lasting change.

You are now ready to tackle the biggest obstacle of all: Your perception of time.

3

MAKING TIME TANGIBLE

We've defined good time management, identified at least one activity you'd like to add back into your schedule, and examined what might be holding you back. So what's next? What makes time so difficult to manage?

After almost two decades as a professional organizer, I've found that the single most common obstacle people face in managing their days lies in *the way they view time*. Therefore, one of the first steps in taking control of time is to challenge your very perception of it.

Most people think of time as intangible. In the journey from chaos to order, it is often easier to organize space than time, because space is something you can actually see. Stacks of papers, piles of clothing, and shelves full of knickknacks are visible. You can pick things up and move them around in your space to see how they fit.

Time, on the other hand, is completely invisible—it's something you feel, and it feels . . . utterly amorphous. How long is a day? Well, that depends on your energy and how much sleep you had. How long is an hour? Well, if you're doing something you love, it whizzes by; but if you're caught up in something dreadful, it crawls painfully along.

As long as time remains slippery and elusive, you will have difficulty managing your days. To be successful, you need to change your perception of time. You need to learn to see time in more visual, measurable terms.

In my own journey to getting organized, my biggest breakthrough came when I realized that organizing time really is no different than organizing space. Let's compare a cluttered closet to a cluttered schedule. What similarities do you see?

"BEFORE"

Cluttered Closet

- Limited amount of space
- More stuff than room to store it
- Items jammed into any available pocket of space, in no particular order
- Haphazard arrangement, making it difficult to see what you have

Cluttered Schedule

- Limited amount of hours
- More tasks than time to do them
- Tasks jammed into any available pocket of time, in no particular order
- Haphazard arrangement, making it difficult to see what you have to do

Essentially, just as a closet is a limited space into which you must fit a certain number of objects, a schedule is a limited number of hours into which you must fit a certain number of tasks. When you start thinking about it this way, time isn't so intangible after all. In fact, each day is simply a container, a storage unit that has a finite capacity. You can only fit so much into it.

If an overstuffed closet and overstuffed schedule are similar, then you could apply the same organizing strategy to each, right? Let's compare an organized closet and an organized day. What similarities do you see?

"AFTER"

Organized Closet

- Similar items are grouped together
- No guesswork as to where to put things
- Orderly arrangement makes most of space

Organized Schedule

- Similar tasks are grouped together
- No guesswork as to when to do things
- Orderly arrangement makes most of day

- You can see what's there at a glance
- Easy to see when you've reached capacity
- Maintain order with one in/one out rule

- You can see what has to be done at a glance
- Easy to see when you've reached capacity
- Maintain order with one in/one out rule

Once you understand that time is a container, you begin to look at your to-dos differently. Essentially, each task is an object that you must find space for in your schedule. Just as every pair of shoes you place in your closet takes up a certain amount of room, each task takes up a certain amount of time. It becomes critical to evaluate your to-dos in terms of their size (duration) in order to determine whether or not they will fit into your schedule. Arranging your day becomes a mathematical equation.

"HOW LONG WILL IT TAKE?"—THE CRITICAL QUESTION

Open up your current to-do list and take a look at it. How many of your tasks have a time estimate next to them? If you are like the majority of people, probably none. (If you do have time estimates—good for you. You might want to skip right to chapter 4.)

When writing out to-do lists, most people only ask themselves one question—WHAT do I need to do? This approach usually results in an intimidating list that goes on for three, four, even five pages. "Register car, do taxes, update résumé, paint the hallway, call Aunt Ethel, buy groceries, etc., etc., etc."

In looking at the list, you may ponder how you feel about each task—"I like this one," "I hate that one"—but you probably don't consider how long it will take. You are approaching your tasks qualitatively, not quantitatively.

The difference between good and bad time managers pivots on the asking of this critical question: How long will it take? Good time managers calculate how long things take and build the time they need into their schedules. People who are good at estimating how long things take aren't born with magical powers, though they may be more mathematically inclined than you and I. Yet, once you understand the concept, it's a simple skill anyone with a calculator can master.

My brother, Steve, is one of the best time managers I know. He got through his demanding medical school studies by using extremely impressive calculating skills. At the beginning of each semester, he'd figure out how many pages he had to read for each course. Then he'd calculate: "It takes me an hour to read, highlight, and study ten pages. I've got six five-hundred-page textbooks to read this semester, that's a total of three thousand pages to read. At ten pages per hour, I'll need three hundred hours to get through. With twelve weeks in the semester, that means I need to study five hours a night if I want to take weekends off."

Perhaps this seems like going overboard. But imagine how relaxed Steve felt knowing that as long as he studied fifty pages a night, he'd make his goal. If he missed a night, he had enough wiggle room to make up for it on another night or the weekend. By breaking the project into a series of manageable steps, the task no longer loomed so massively over his head. No pressure, less stress, no surprises.

Calculating how long things take is not a mysterious talent. It is a skill anyone can master. It may take you two weeks of practice to get the hang of it, but you can, without a doubt, learn this critical skill. I'm going to show you how on the following pages.

WHY DON'T WE ASK THIS QUESTION?

We often resist calculating how long things will take for fear of discovering that we actually don't have enough time to do it all. Better close our eyes, jump in, and hope for the best.

Other times we miscalculate based on wishful thinking—we believe if we are extra disciplined and diligent, we can get things done more quickly than usual.

My response? Denial doesn't change reality. Things take as long as they take. If you ignore the truth, you may very well run out of time before you've even started what's most important.

If you consistently miscalculate, you'll constantly be taking on more than you can handle. You'll start each day with tremendous ambition, only to feel defeated by the end of the day. Miscalculating tasks can also lead to procrastination—if you think a half-hour task will take two hours, you'll never get started.

GETTING REAL

Writing Client Reports

When I first started my business, at the end of every initial consultation with a client, I'd present a verbal assessment and plan of action. "Here's where you are, here's where you want to go, and here are the six steps that will get you there. It will take approximately x number of hours to get the job done, at an hourly rate of y."

The clients would nod their heads, love the plan, tell me it made perfect sense. Then they'd ask the killer question: Are you going to send me a written report? Wanting to please, I'd say, "Sure," and put it on my to-do list for the next day.

I'd sit down at my desk the next morning, full of vim and vigor, determined to cross the report off my to-do list in an hour or two. Inevitably, by 3 p.m., I'd still be toiling away. By the end of the day, I'd finally be finished. Unfortunately, I never got to the other fifteen items on my to-do list for that day.

The next time a client asked for a report, I'd say yes, again. Again, it'd take me all day. What was wrong with me, I wondered? This shouldn't take so long!

I decided to take a closer look at myself. For the next five Needs Assessment Reports, I timed the task and consistently, no matter what I did, it took me between five and six hours to complete each one! Why? Given my perfectionistic tendencies, I'd belabor the language, experiment with fonts, fiddle with the margins, rethink the closing. I wished it took less time, but like it or not, this was just how long it took me, Julie Morgenstern, to write a report.

Once I faced reality, I was in a position to make a thoughtful decision. Spending that much time writing a report that the client had already bought into verbally didn't seem like the best use of my time as a business owner. So, what choices did I have? I could

1. charge the clients for the time to write reports
2. streamline the process using templates and standard wording
3. hire someone else to write the reports from my notes
4. say no

Ultimately, I decided to just say no. I figured that since my clients were already disorganized and overwhelmed, I wasn't serving them very well by allowing them to postpone the decision to get organized, or sending them another piece of paper to get lost in the piles on their desk. If my diagnosis and plan of action made sense to them at the initial consultation, we should schedule the plan, collect a retainer, and get started. It worked, and my business flourished.

The point is, once I was dealing with the facts—as they were, not as I thought they should be—I was in a position to solve the problem. I made a conscious choice to avoid getting caught in a time trap of my own making.

That is why asking the question "How long will this take?" of every single task you do is the number one gateway skill to good time management.

Unfortunately, it's easy to dramatically under- or overestimate how long tasks take based on how we feel about something. Hate doing the dishes? It must take an hour. Love surfing the net? Easy, it'll only take ten minutes. We often miscalculate tasks that we don't enjoy doing. Look at the following list of tasks that people tend to procrastinate on. How long do you think it takes you to do each one?

Task	Your Time Estimate
Pay bills	
Write thank-you note	
Write business letter	
Pack/unpack before/after a trip	
Daily filing	
Hook up new electronic device	

It takes different people different amounts of time to do the identical task. In a survey I conducted on my Web site, I asked participants to estimate "how long it took" them to complete the tasks listed above. Two thousand people responded. Here are the results.

Pay bills

34%   16–30 min.
29%   31 min. to 1 hr.

20%   1–15 min.
14%   Over 1 hr.

Write a thank-you note

70%   1–15 min.
22%   16–30 min.
5%   31 min. to 1 hr.
4%   Over 1 hr.

Write a business letter

42%   16–30 min.
25%   31 min. to 1 hr.
17%   1–15 min.
7%   Over 1 hr.

Pack/unpack before/after a trip

33%   1–3 hrs.
33%   31 min. to 1 hr.
17%   16–30 min.
12%   Over 3 hrs.
3%   1–15 min.

Daily filing

44%   1–15 min.
28%   16–30 min.
14%   31 min. to 1 hr.
5%   Over 1 hr.

Hook up new electronic device

29%   31 min. to 1 hr.
27%   16–30 min.

21%   Over 1 hr.
20%   1–15 min.

Compare your estimates to those above and you can see that tasks that take you just a few minutes may take other people hours. Why? We all have different skill sets, interests, concentration cycles, and energy levels. The key is to find out how long it really takes YOU to do the things you need to do and move away from wishful thinking. Once you know how long it takes you to do something, you may decide it's a better use of the world's resources to have someone else do it—that's what I call good time management.

IMPROVING YOUR OWN ESTIMATING SKILLS

As best you can, try to be literal when you make a time estimate. So many of us are in the habit of saying, "that'll take two seconds," whether we're talking about getting dressed, making a call, or running to the store. Silly as it may seem, this affects the way we think about time. If you break this habit and start paying attention to how long it really takes, you'll find it's much easier to accomplish all you want to do.

Here are two exercises to help you become a better time estimator.

Exercise #1: Target Three Tasks

Choose three tasks you tend to procrastinate on, and study yourself. Create a chart with three columns. It should look like this:

Time Estimating Log

Task	Your Estimation of How Long It Will Take	How Long It Actually Took
Submit expense reports		
Do the dishes		
Pay bills		

Time yourself doing each task at least three times to get a solid average. If your times vary dramatically, did you approach the task at different times of day? That could affect your energy or ability to concentrate.

Exercise #2: Keep Track in Your Daily Planner

For one week, next to each item you put on your to-do list, jot down how long you think it will take. Then, when you do the task, time yourself, and write down the actual time it took to complete it. Your list may look like this:

Planner Page

Task	Estimated Time	Actual Time
Make dinner reservations	(10 min.)	5 min.
Write thank-you note	(15 min.)	45 min.
Create party invitation	(1 hr.)	3 hrs.
Pay bills	(30 min.)	Didn't do
Make doctor's appointment	(5 min.)	Didn't do

Task	Estimated Time	Actual Time
Fix bicycle	(30 min.)	1 hr.—still broken
Back up computer	(15 min.)	1 hr.
Plan weekly meeting at work	(15 min.)	30 min.
Write speech	(3 hrs.)	2 hrs. 30 min.

Compare your estimates to the actuals. Do you see a pattern? Are your estimates always off by the same percentage? Are there certain types of tasks you find harder to judge than others (e.g., ones that involve writing, or dealing with other people.)? Are there some tasks that went much more quickly than you thought they would? What does that tell you about your relationship to that task?

In one week, you might not have gotten to all the kinds of tasks you routinely do. Or you might not feel you have a handle on this skill yet. If either of those things is true, use this tool for up to a month. Master it. Make it your own. It's worth the effort. Once you get good at this skill, you will be able to schedule your time much more realistically.

You also won't have to be this detailed forever. After two weeks to a month of concerted effort, you won't have to estimate the time required for each and every five-minute task on your list. You'll develop a keen sense of how many calls you can fit into a morning, or how long it takes to pay the bills each week.

GETTING REAL

Fixing the Garbage Disposal

Beth's garbage disposal had been broken for eight months. She was sure all it needed was a fifteen-minute adjustment and was embarrassed that she had put off such a quick job for so long. I challenged her fifteen-minute estimate.

Do you know how to fix it? I asked. No, Beth said, but I think it just needs a minor adjustment. I can read the manual. *Do you know where the manual is?* Well, no, I'll have to look for it. *Do you have the tools required?* Beth wasn't sure.

How long will it take to fix the garbage disposal?

Find the manual	30 min.
Read the manual	15 min.
Search toolbox for proper-size screw	15 min.
Shop at hardware store to buy proper screw	30 min.
Make adjustment to disposal	15 min.
Clean up	30 min.
TOTAL TIME	**135 min.**
	(2 hrs. 15 min.)

So, it wasn't a fifteen-minute project after all! And somewhere deep down Beth knew it, which was the real reason why she'd procrastinated for eight months. Once she faced the reality, she realized she wasn't the best person for the job. She bartered with her brother-in-law, an experienced do-it-yourselfer who had the knowledge and the tools ready. For him, it actually was a fifteen-minute job. Her part of the bargain? Cooking his favorite meal and inviting him to family dinner.

Hidden Time Costs

When you are calculating, you need to factor in a variety of hidden time costs. Here are a few of the most commonly overlooked ones. Acknowledging them will improve your estimating skills from the start.

- **Travel Time, To and From**

Take into consideration when and how you are traveling. Are you traveling at rush hour? Are you taking public transportation? How reliable is it? Do you have to leave extra time in case the train is late? What is the parking situation? If you are going to an office building with an elevator, remember to leave time for waiting for the elevator, walking down the hall, and talking to the receptionist. If your appointment is for 10 a.m., and you've timed it so you walk in the door of the building at 10 a.m., you're going to be late.

- **Setup Time**

Do you need time to gather materials? Do you need to lay them out? Do you need to get yourself oriented to the project? Do you need to change your clothes (to work out, for example)?

- **Cleanup/Wind-Down time**

You need time to put everything away. Also, if you're leaving a task before it's completed, you need time to write a little note for yourself so when you go back, you know where you left off.

- **Stewing Time**

Some tasks require thinking time. You might need to think before you start, or you might need stewing time during the project. This time needs to be built in.

• **Interruption Time**

Is there a chance you'll be interrupted? If you'll be doing the task during a time of day when you're likely to be interrupted, or if you've got kids around, build in extra time so that an interruption or two doesn't throw your entire schedule off.

• **Unexpected-Problems Time**

A good time manager builds in time for the event that things don't go smoothly. Since few things go off without a hitch, add a little cushion to deal with complications that arise. When in doubt about how much cushion time you'll need, factor in 20 percent.

• **Refreshment Time**

You need to break for moving around or stretching. You also need breaks for meals, snacks, drinks, and an occasional trip to the loo. Don't forget to build this time in as well.

MULTITASKING SLOWS YOU DOWN

Once thought to boost productivity, multitasking has been discovered to slow you down. If you are one of those people who effectively switches between ten projects at once, but finishes everything by the end of the day, you probably do have an innate sense of how long things take. No need to change that behavior— it's working for you.

But for most people, working in a scattered way makes it difficult to get back on track, and they end their day with many projects started and nothing complete. Even more damaging, multitasking this way makes it impossible to accurately estimate how long tasks take, so you are in no position to plan your day wisely.

GETTING REAL

Multitasking Prevents Proper Calculating

Carol had a hard time estimating how long tasks took, because she was always doing ten things at once. She'd sit down at 9 a.m. to prepare a presentation for an upcoming meeting and while working on it field five phone calls, respond to twenty e-mails, and chat with three coworkers. By 5 p.m., she finished the presentation but had no idea how long it actually took her to do it.

If you would like to boost your productivity, and increase your ability to calculate tasks accurately, you need to develop your tolerance for concentration. Start by blocking off fifteen minutes at a time, and force yourself to do only one task till the fifteen minutes are up. If you aren't finished yet, add another fifteen minutes. You can keep coming back to the task—but each time you work on it, focus 100 percent for fifteen minutes. Add up the totals by the end of the day.

Once you can concentrate for fifteen minutes, you can increase your time to thirty minutes at a time, then forty-five, and eventually stretch it to an hour, if you can.

This is a huge behavior change, and it will be challenging. Yet once you discover your true set point for concentration (be it fifteen, thirty, forty-five, or sixty minutes), your productivity will soar. You can break down all of your tasks into appropriate-sized pieces, know how long things take, and feel a sense of accomplishment you've never felt before.

ESTIMATING TIME FOR BIG PROJECTS

What if you're faced with a big project? How do you estimate how long that will take? Think back to the way my brother Steve approached his study schedule. Break the project down into its steps. Pull out your calculator and your courage.

Do this for any big project, whether you're decorating your house, planning a party, starting a business, or buying a computer. Know your starting date and your target date or deadline. Break the big project into its component parts. Don't be afraid to figure out how much time for each step. Ask others who've done similar projects before how much time it took them. Do a little research and planning before you start so that you don't come up short on time. Once you break it down, you'll see that you don't have to deal with the whole monster—deal with the smaller segments.

Project

Study market trends and present findings to the board of directors.
Deadline: 1 month

Steps	How Long Will It Take?
1. Define scope of the project	3 hrs.
2. Research trends	8 hrs.
3. Think and assimilate material	8 hrs.
4. Draft report	4 hrs.
5. Edit report	2 hrs.
6. Polish report	1 hr.
7. Practice presentation	45 min.
8. Get your handouts ready	15 min.

Project

Plan Retirement Party
Deadline: June 12

Task	How Long Will It Take?
Plan guest list	1 hr.
Price catering halls	2 afternoons
Reserve catering hall	1 hr.
Compile addresses	3 hrs.
Buy invitations	1 hr.
Prepare and send invitations	2 hrs.
Finalize arrangements	1 hr.

How Long It Takes Other People

Once you get the hang of estimating tasks, you will realize that other people may not be so good at it. When someone makes a request for your time, or wants to get together, start talking in terms of how much is needed. If a colleague interrupts you to talk to you about a new project, find out if it will take five minutes, or thirty; then either accept the interruption, or schedule a time to talk about it later, when it's more convenient.

If a friend calls you in the middle of your evening with your family, ask how much time she needs so that you can honestly determine if you have the time right now to give her the focus she really requires. If you don't have that amount of time at the moment, set up a time to call her back when you can really listen.

You also raise the other person's awareness of time by bringing up how much time you've got at the beginning of a conversation. For example, "I've got fifteen minutes before the kids get home (or the staff meeting starts). Can we cover the issue in that abount of time?" The interrupter is more likely to get straight to the point, and if he begins rambling when the time is up, it will be easier for you to cut him short.

People will respect you for setting boundaries, and may even become better at time estimating themselves—no more asking you, "Got a second?"

Of course some people swear, no matter what the circumstances, that they only need five minutes, but inevitably keep you talking for thirty minutes or more. What do you do about that? Just as you have to work with who you are, you also have to work with who the people around you are.

Study the people you live and work with, and accept the quirkiness of their habits. You are responsible for your own schedule. If Jonathan always takes forty-five minutes—even though he always asks for ten—don't expect him to change. Consider his stated request for ten minutes as a real request for forty-five. Then decide if you will give him the time.

GETTING REAL

Becky, Mom with Two Kids

Becky called me for help with conquering the morning madness in her household. It took six wake-up attempts before her son, Benji, would finally roll out of bed. Her daughter, Sara, always realized her outfit was completely wrong just as they headed out the door. As a result, getting her two kids ready and off to school was tense, chaotic, and stressful, and they always left late.

Becky tried every trick in the book to improve her kids' morning behavior. She told Benji he could play a video game before school if he got up when she first tried to roust him. She had Sara choose her outfit the night before. Nothing helped.

I suggested that Becky stop fighting her kids' habits. Being surprised and annoyed by it every day was not helping the situation. For one week, she timed them. Every morning, the six wake-up attempts meant it took a total of thirty minutes for Benji to get out of bed. And each last-minute changing of clothes took Sara fifteen minutes.

All Becky had to do to restore calm in the morning was to get real, adjusting the wake-up and exit times to accommodate how long it really took her kids to get ready. She set Benji's alarm to ring thirty minutes before he actually had to get up. And to outsmart Sara's last-minute inevitable clothes-changing scene, they left for school fifteen minutes earlier. This way, when Sara panicked and insisted on changing, the cushion time was already built in.

By acknowledging her kids' quirks, Becky could build in time for everyone to get ready at their pace. There were no more fights and no more lateness.

BUILDING ON YOUR GATEWAY SKILL

Mastering the skill of estimating tasks is the number one gateway skill to good time management. Once you grasp the concept of time as a container, you'll want to make sure each thing you put into the closet of your day is meaningful, important, and rewarding to you. And you will be motivated to develop other time-management skills as well, such as creating shortcuts for routine tasks, delegating, and mastering the diplomatic art of saying no.

Now that we've covered the basics, you can build on your new view of time in a couple of ways.

If you are so overwhelmed with to-dos that you can barely breathe, never mind thinking about big-picture goals, go to part 2. The "Quick-Start Program" will help you get a fast grip on your days, to generate the breathing room you need to begin thinking about the bigger picture.

Ultimately, time management is about life management—and true freedom comes from stepping back from the daily grind to Analyze, Strategize, and Attack your time-management frustrations on a global level. Parts 3, 4, and 5 will enable you to build on your new view of time to design a life that fulfills your goals and allows you to manage the daily onslaught of choices and interruptions with confidence, clarity, and satisfaction.

Here we go. . . .

PART II

QUICK-START
PROGRAM

4

THE WADE FORMULA

OK, take a deep breath.

You've made it to part 2—a section dedicated to putting you in control, fast. If you are drowning in a tidal wave of tasks with no time or perspective to think about the bigger picture, the quick-start program was written with you in mind.

This chapter and chapter 5 are a lifeline that will give you the breathing room you need to approach time management from a calmer, more centered place. Once you've gotten yourself out from under the piles, you'll have more time in your schedule (and space in your head) to tackle the broader, deeper time-management issues of parts 3, 4, and 5.

There are two steps to giving yourself this much needed breathing room:

1. Managing your gargantuan to-do list
2. Conquering paper clutter

The quick-start program will help you make the shift from reactive to proactive by giving you the basic skills to get out from under the pileup. This chapter teaches you the rapid WADE Formula to quickly take charge of the overwhelming number of to-dos that are constantly flying at you. The next chapter describes a three-step program for getting on top of the time backlog represented by the piles of paper in your life.

When I speak to large audiences about taking charge of their time, there are always a few hands that shoot up to tell me I just don't understand. They can't take charge of their time! Someone else—a micromanaging boss, a job that was once handled by three people, a newborn baby—dictates what gets done and when. To them I say: You can turn the tables on the situation; you just need a few skills in your pocket. The WADE Formula is the first step toward getting back in the driver's seat and taking charge of your time. Bring it on.

MANAGING THE DAILY ONSLAUGHT

With so little time, how do you choose between the huge number of tasks you face on any given day? The WADE Formula helps you sort and separate the overwhelming pileup of demands.

Here's the formula:

WRITE IT DOWN—record everything you have to do in one reliable location—your planner or to-do pad.

ADD IT UP—Estimate how long each task will take. Break large projects down into small parts for easier calculation.

DECIDE what you will actually do. If overloaded, you can elect to apply the four D's—delete, delay, delegate, or diminish them into smaller, shorter tasks.

EXECUTE YOUR PLAN—Put your plan into action without being hindered by procrastination or perfectionism.

We'll go through each of these steps, one by one, in detail. Can you already see how you might use the WADE Formula in your daily life?

Write It Down

You can't rely on your memory when it comes to remembering everything you need to do—there's just too much!

Write everything you have to do in one consistent location, like your planner or a master to-do list, *not* on a patchwork of Post-its, napkins, and scraps of paper. Don't just write down meetings and appointments, it's important to record every task, phone call, and project. Once you get into the habit of writing everything down in a single consistent location, you'll stop worrying that you're forgetting something—and you can actually concentrate on getting things done.

Where do you actually write this list? Generally speaking, I am not a fan of master to-do lists. Master to-do lists are like a big pile that easily becomes overwhelming. When your list goes on for seven pages, you can spend fifteen minutes just trying to figure out what to do next! And you never feel all that productive because no matter what you get done, you still have six and a half pages of to-dos left at the end of each day. At this point, however, my preferences shouldn't stop you from recording everything you need to get done. If a master list is the best starting point for you, go for it.

Once you have a system in place, my preference is that you write your to-dos down in your planner, on the day you intend to do them. Need to shop for a birthday gift? Ask yourself when you will do it and then turn to that page in your planner (e.g., Saturday) and make a note: "shop for Kylie's gift." If you need help selecting the best planner for you, turn to chapter 6.

Some people prefer to keep their master to-do lists in a section in the back of their paper planner, organized by category. You might allot one page for long-term work projects, one for friends and family, and another for chores and errands. This allows you to capture every idea that occurs to you. With an electronic planner, use the to-do list function to categorize each entry by area of life. In any case you will eventually have to go back to the list to designate a specific day and time when you intend to do each task.

Add It Up

You know from chapter 3 that every day is a container that can only fit a certain number of tasks. So, you need to go beyond the question "What do I need to do?" and ask, "How long will it take?" Write an estimate of how long each task will take, then add up the time. (For help in accurately estimating how long tasks take, go back to chapter 3.)

Is there enough room in your schedule for all that needs to be done? If you only have four open hours, but have scheduled 5.75 hours' worth of tasks, you need to make a few adjustments, which brings you to the next step. Decide.

Decide

In most cases, once you add up your tasks you'll discover that you have many more tasks than time available. When you reach the limits of your time, you need to make some quick decisions. Use the four Ds to create a more doable plan.

The Four Ds: Delete, Delay, Diminish, Delegate

DELETE TASKS: For those of us who want to do everything and be everywhere, we need to make an effort to distinguish between what's truly important and what's not so crucial or urgent. Come on, do you really need to *rearrange your pencil drawer* the day before you go on a business trip? Must you call your friend to gossip about nothing at all? Is it imperative that you rebind all your photo albums just to make them look prettier? Which tasks are you doing simply out of habit? What tasks do you say yes to, that you'd rather not do at all? There's a certain amount of psychology involved in "deleting" tasks, or saying no—those will be addressed in depth in chapter 12, "Purge." For now, just take a hard look at your list and answer the question: What absolutely does not have to get done right now? Would your life change drastically, or would anyone else be hurt if these things don't get done? If the answer is no, cross them off your list. Then, breathe a sigh of relief.

DELAY TASKS: Even if you've determined that a task or activity is important, ask yourself, "Can it wait?" Can it be postponed until another hour, day, or week? Remember, we all tend to gravitate toward tasks we enjoy or consider easy, and away from the tougher, more important tasks. Reorganizing your recipe files is probably a good idea, but do you have to do it on the one day you need to prepare for house guests, work overtime, and go to your kid's soccer game? Moreover, just because someone asks you to do something the moment they think of it doesn't mean it's urgent. Perhaps they just wanted to get it off their own lists (even though the deadline isn't for several days). If you're particularly pressed for time, try to delay some of your ongoing to-dos until your schedule opens up.

DIMINISH TASKS: Provided you're a responsible person who takes your obligations seriously, diminishing your workload is not about doing a hack job or cheating—it's about becoming a more efficient person.

If you're a perfectionist, you might approach every single task with the intention of getting a perfect 10. But when time is limited, you need to be able to find the quickest way to your goal. By investing a few hours creating streamlined systems for routine tasks, and skipping certain steps of onetime projects, you can eliminate a lot of grunt work and save time in the long run. See "How to do Anything Faster" later in this chapter for shortcuts to routine tasks to get you started.

DELEGATE TASKS: Knowing how to delegate effectively is one of the most important and valuable time management skills. It's also one of the most psychologically loaded (for more on that, see chapter 12, "Purge"). Like diminishing tasks, delegating is not something you do to avoid your responsibilities; it's a technique you use to fulfill them.

Effective delegation builds teamwork. It creates a situation in which each team member is doing the task that best complements his or her abilities and talents, freeing everyone to make his or her greatest contribution. Ask yourself, "Is there someone who could do this faster, better, or well enough?" If so, give it up. There are two main things to consider when delegating: (1) what to delegate, and (2) whom to delegate to. See the "Optimizing Resources" section later in this chapter for quick help with delegating.

EXECUTE YOUR PLAN

There's an old saying: "Plan your work, then work your plan." There's no point to making a plan if you aren't going to implement it. This means completing the tasks you set forth on the days you decided to do them. It also means starting and finishing projects when you say you will. Read chapter 14, "Containerize," to learn more about psychological ways to control procrastination and overly perfectionist tendencies.

GETTING REAL

Julie, Applying the WADE Formula in Action

I was not always an organized person. My daughter's birth in 1985 inspired me to get it together because I realized that my poor innocent babe would never see the light of day if I didn't get organized.

Having mastered spatial organizing before time, I had the opportunity to see just how far I'd come with my organizing skills when Jessi was a young teenager. Less than two weeks before her bat mitzvah (kind of like a cross between a huge sweet sixteen, a wedding, and a confirmation, it was a huge affair that, as a single parent, I coordinated by myself), I got the call every author dreams of—it was *The Oprah Winfrey Show*. They wanted to know if I was available to coordinate a big spring cleanup of their production offices and several viewers' homes for an upcoming show. Fantastic! When did they want to do this? All within the next ten days!

Was I ready to jump at this incredible opportunity? Was I organized enough to manage all of the details involved in pulling off both the bat mitzvah and the *Oprah* show simultaneously? The answer was a resounding yes. Here's how the WADE Formula came to my rescue:

W: Because everything I had to do for Jessi's big event was already written out, it was relatively easy to do a quick scan to see exactly where I stood. To that list, I added all of the tasks I'd need to do in connection with the show: coordinate travel, review photos of the spaces to be organized, order products, restock supply kit, assemble support staff, figure out what to wear, get a manicure, plan my presentation.

A: After adding up all my tasks, it was clear that I had many more tasks than time to do them in. Fortunately, I had the four Ds to bail me out.

D: I deleted every task I could. For example, I decided that it was fine to wear clothes I already owned for the taping, instead of going shopping, but I knew that the manicure was a must. Once I viewed the photos of the spaces to be organized, I'd generate a list of products to be ordered and delegate the product ordering and shipping to someone on my staff. I delegated the assembling of the written program for Jessi's ceremony to a dear friend. And of course, I delayed every nonurgent project unrelated to the show or bat mitzvah until after these two events were over.

E: My suitcase was packed in a flash and I was on the next plane to Harpo Studios in Chicago. During that whirlwind two weeks, my planner kept me very focused on everything I had to do and every place I had to be. My files and database were very organized, so the information I needed for both events was at my fingertips. I didn't miss a beat.

Instead of missing the moment, I was able to embrace this unexpected convergence of priorities. The result was one of the most glorious weeks in my life—celebrating a momentous, spiritual occasion with my daughter, and appearing on the most coveted TV show in the world. Here's to the power of the WADE Formula!

HOW TO DO ANYTHING FASTER

Now that you've got the gist of the WADE Formula, use the tips and ideas below to spur your thinking about what shortcuts and streamlined tasks might work for you.

Errands and Chores

- **Create a master shopping list.** Organize it according to your grocery store's layout. Make copies, and keep one posted on your refrigerator, so that as you run out of items, you simply check off what you need. When it's time to go shopping, simply grab the list and go. (This works with office supplies, too.)
- **Order groceries online.** Www.Peapod.com and www.Fresh Direct.com are two reputable Web sites worth investigating. If you're wary of purchasing produce and meat over the Internet, buy only canned goods, paper products, and boxed items, saving everything else for your local grocery store. You'll still save time because (1) you won't spend waiting in line; and (2) shopping online is faster—there aren't as many tempting distractions!
- **Cook faster. Get a crock pot.** Toss ingredients in before you head out for the day, and come home to a fully cooked meal. Or, get a book on thirty-minute meals, and choose fourteen dinner ideas to rotate every two weeks. If you love to cook, use weekends for your more creative meals.
- **Reduce the clutter.** According to cleaning professionals, eliminating clutter can reduce housework by as much as 40 percent!
- **Deep-clean rooms in rotation.** You might decide that every Wednesday you'll clean the bathroom and every Friday you'll clean the kitchen. When you clean just one room at a time, you don't waste time running from one room to the next, or constantly looking for time to clean your house. (*If you can afford it, hire someone to do the deep-cleaning. Then you just have to make time for daily pickups!*)
- **Team-clean your house with the kids.** Cleaning as a family is another way to make a semiarduous chore into a fun family activity. Attack each room as a unit (instead of sending one person to the bathroom and another to vacuum the living room) and see

how long it takes you to clean the entire house. Set a regular day (like Saturday) for the team clean, and rotate who gets each job. You never know—in a few weeks, your kids could be lining up to use the DustBuster!

- **Be prepared for spontaneous shopping opportunities.** Assign a separate page in the back of your planner or an errand notebook for each of your family members, yourself, and your home. Keep a running list of what each person needs on his or her own page (e.g., get poster board for Jimmy, pick up developed film at camera shop)—and you'll make the most of every spontaneous shopping opportunity.

- **Speed up laundry.** Set up your laundry space to include a table for folding clothes and a rod with empty hangers so you can hang clothes as soon as they come out of the dryer (and avoid as much ironing as possible!). Assign a basket for each family member (color-coding is one option: Ned—blue, Jake—red, Will—green, Hannah—purple) and make each one responsible for collecting his or her stuff and putting it away. Always buy the same style and color socks—you'll save a lot of time matching up pairs.

Getting Out the Door

- **Lay out clothes the night before.** This is a real time and stress saver for those who change outfits or accessories three times before walking out the door each morning. Ease the pressure by selecting and ironing (if necessary) your clothes and accessories (tie, belt, jewelry, scarf) the night before, when your head is clear and relaxed.

- **Post a "Remember to Take" checklist by your front door.** Review it before leaving the house (e.g., "Remember to take your wallet, keys, planner, checkbook, umbrella, kids' backpacks, homework, ballet shoes, soccer equipment, cell phone, and charger"). Create a game with your kids—before you walk out the door, have everyone line up for a verbal check. "Homework?" "Check!" "Soccer stuff?" "Check!" Laminate the list and hang it on the inside of your coat closet.

- **Create an "Errand Center" by the door.** Drop clothes for the dry cleaner, packages for the post office, books for the library, items to return to friends, in the same spot, to prevent frantic searches. A shelf can serve as "Repair Center" for clothes that need mending, toys that need batteries, and items that need gluing.

Paying Bills

- **Pay bills online.** Though the idea of this makes some people nervous, once you have tried online banking, you'll never go back. After entering the mailing and account information for the people you write checks to every month (which can take thirty to forty-five minutes), paying bills takes all of five minutes. No stamps, no check writing, no worries. Security is excellent on these sites. Since the balances are "real-time," if someone has done any tampering with your account—which can happen whether you bank online or not—you'll discover errors more quickly.
- **Pay bills over the phone, via credit card.** This is great for people who get air miles with every credit charge purchase: Pay your bills via credit card for six months, and you could earn a trip to Italy!
- **Set up automatic payments for regular bills.** Just don't forget to make sure there's enough in your account to cover the bills, and deduct the amount from your check register.
- **Pay bills once or twice a month.** Gather your bills, write the check for each one, seal and stamp the envelope. Indicate on the back of each one, in pencil, the date it needs to be mailed out. Send bills out as their dates come up.
- **Create a bill-paying center.** Stock it with everything you need for the job—checks, envelopes, stamps, pens, and a calculator

so you don't have to search for them every time. Keep your receipts and bill-paying records in portable file boxes nearby to prevent a backlog of filing.

Birthdays, Anniversaries, Holidays

- **Buy birthday, holiday, anniversary, and just plain friendship cards for the entire year.** Once a year, or at the beginning of each month, fill out cards, and put a date to mail in the spot where the stamp goes. Store them by the front door, or with your bills to pay, then stamp and mail them out on the date designated on the envelope.
- **Designate a favorite wedding or baby gift and give those signature items every time.** A gorgeous frame, artsy photo album, handcrafted vase, baby blanket, or a basket of your favorite baby books are great choices. (Or, pick one store you can always go to when you need to buy a gift.)
- **Send virtual greeting cards.** Skip the snail-mail card altogether and bookmark a site that sends virtual birthday cards. Electronic greetings are on their way in five minutes' time. A few days before the special day, some services, such as www.Hallmark.com and www.AmericanGreeting.com, will e-mail you a reminder along with a few gift suggestions (which you can order online and send directly to the recipient).

Pack for a Trip

- **Simplify the color scheme of all your clothes.** Working within a color scheme reduces the time you spend thinking, searching, and making decisions about what to wear or what accessories will match your outfits.
- **Make a master travel checklist.** Include on the list categories of clothing, tickets, passports, camera, medicines, toiletries, etc.

You can customize quantities and garment weight according to the length of your trip and climate of your destination.

- **Keep a toiletries bag prepacked.** There's no need to waste time packing toothpaste, a toothbrush, soap, moisturizer, etc., every time you go out of town. A prepacked travel kit that duplicates your standard toiletries is cheap enough and worth the cash in the time and hassle you save.
- **Write or print address labels for people you want to send postcards to,** before leaving on a trip.
- **Make a reminder list of last-minute things to check as you're leaving the house for a trip.** Have you watered the plants, turned on the alarm system, and unplugged any extra appliances?
- **Unpack the moment you get home!** Do not stop, do not collect $200. Before you sit down to open the mail, relax, or listen to your messages, unpack your bag. If you don't do it before dealing with the new stuff, your suitcase will probably sit in the middle of your bedroom, stuffed full of dirty clothes, for a week!

Shortcuts for Writing

- **Create computer templates for documents you find yourself typing over and over.** While you don't want your correspondence to sound like a form letter, writing every letter from scratch is an enormous waste of time. Create templates for pitch letters, proposals, thank-you notes, overdue bill notices, and any other type of document you write regularly. In Microsoft Word, just open a new document, design the form, and save it as a template instead of a document.
- **Keep thank-you notes simple.** Try a three-sentence format that will speed you through the labor of being so inventive. For example:

> *Dear* _____,
>
> *You were so thoughtful / kind / generous / gracious to _____. I am enjoying looking at / wearing / listening to / reading / remembering the _____. It's something I've always wanted. Thank you for thinking of me,*
>
> *Your Name*

- **Do one quick first draft.** Sometimes getting something, anything, on the page is better than nothing. Instead of belaboring each word, sentence, and paragraph, just write whatever comes to mind (even if that's an outline, a few words, or a seemingly incomplete and incoherent idea). Once that's done, you at least have a document to work with, either to revise yourself or to work on with someone else.
- **Track expenses as you go.** No one likes submitting expense reports. Instead of stuffing receipts into various jacket pockets, briefcase compartments, and your car, keep all receipts in a designated envelope for the week or month (depending on when you need to submit them). Record what the expense is actually for on the top of each receipt (e.g., $78.56—client dinner; $36—cab to hotel). Or, keep a running expenses list in your PalmPilot as you go.
- **Skip steps on large projects.** If you are short on time, and have a big project, ask what steps you might be able to skip. Let's say your company is launching a new service. As the project manager, you have one month to hire the new people to actually provide the service, train them, create a brochure, do a mailing, and coordinate a launch party. Are all of those steps absolutely necessary? Maybe you can shortcut the step of developing the

brochure, and instead print a simple postcard inviting people to the launch party to check out a great new service!

Do you have shortcut ideas of your own?

OPTIMIZING RESOURCES

Delegating can be fraught with psychological obstacles, but if you're reading this chapter it's probably because you desperately need to lighten your workload. We'll deal with the psychology of delegating in chapter 12, but for now, let's concentrate on teaching the very pragmatic skill of sharing the workload. If you have a hard time with delegating, try to think of it in terms of optimizing the resources at your command. The exercises below can help you get started.

What to Delegate

Scan your to-do list and ask yourself where your time is best spent; consider your talents, vision, skills, and preferences. Where's your greatest contribution? What can only you do? Which tasks best serve your goals?

Exercise #1: List those tasks here and keep them for yourself.

_____

_____

_____

Once you've determined what you should *never* delegate, look at your list again. Ask yourself if there's any remaining task that someone else could do better, as well, or good enough? Delegate any tasks you aren't good at, don't enjoy, or find detrimental to your time and energy (that you need for higher-priority activities). Think about the routine tasks you do (e.g., write client reports, coordinate mass mailings, track media clips). Would it save you time in the long run to teach someone else how to do those tasks? What about onetime projects? Is there anything about those projects that someone else might be interested in learning about? How would you benefit from delegating the project to that person?

Review your list of remaining tasks and double-check that none of them are simply unnecessary. If a task doesn't need to be done at all, don't delegate it—just eliminate it.

Exercise #2: What tasks can you delegate?

_____

_____

_____

Whom to Delegate To

You may be surprised how many people are available to help. The real key is to have everyone do what he or she is best at.

- **Staff.** Are you giving your staff everything they are capable of? Explore their talents and give people a chance to make a contribution. Are you holding on to any tasks, just because you're used to doing them, or because you feel bad giving them to someone else? Especially in lean times, they might balk at being handed an additional project—they already feel overloaded! It's your job to help them prioritize. Help them determine where to spend their time.
- **Coworker.** Delegating to coworkers can be tricky—they're in the same situation you are: too much to do, not enough time. Assuming you can't give them any of your work, what about making a trade? If you're a whiz at Excel, and your cube-mate

is an expert when it comes to setting up e-mail filters, try to work out a fair exchange. You'll both benefit.

Boss. You might not be able to delegate directly to your boss, but he or she may be able to help and significantly speed the plow. If your boss asks you to do a task that would take two hours without his input, but twenty minutes with it, speak up. Chances are, he'll give you twenty minutes of his time, so you can complete the task and get back to other critical assignments.

Outside Service. Hire movers to pack, or caterers to prepare and serve refreshments at a party. Delegate the part of the job that is the least familiar to you. You don't always want to spend time learning a new skill to finish a project. Let someone else figure out how to keep the appetizers warm on the way from point A to point B.

Family Member. If in trying to do it all, you feel constantly overwhelmed, you won't have enough energy to make your most important contribution to your family—providing love, listening, and showing an interest in each family member. When the whole family contributes to the work of running the household, it brings you closer together and helps your kids learn valuable skills. So, engage them in cooking, cleaning, grocery shopping, gardening, running errands, etc.—it'll take the pressure off of you, but it's also a great way to spend some productive, quality time together.

Friend. If you have a friend who loves shopping (and you hate it!), give her the green light to buy clothes for you whenever she happens upon something during a spree of her own. If she hates gardening but loves flowers (and the garden is your passion!), make a fair trade. You can also share cooking and carpool responsibilities. Use each other's strengths to benefit you both—hey, that's what friends are for!

Exercise #3: What can you delegate? Whom can you delegate to?

Task	Who
_____	_____
_____	_____
_____	_____

GETTING REAL

Regan, Sales Manager, Single Working Mom

Regan's head was spinning—a busy, single working mom, she spent her days running from one task to the next. She didn't know how to reduce her workload. The last time she asked her twelve-year-old daughter Tracy to do the laundry, Tracy accidentally flooded the basement!

How could she delegate her household chores? I asked her to list everything that needed doing, give each task a time estimate, and decide who in her household would be the best person for the job. Even if they didn't do each thing perfectly, sharing the labor would bring them closer as a family, and free up Regan's time to relax with her kids.

Goal: Clean, inviting home

Task	Time Estimate	Best Person
Daily pickup	15 min./day	Whole family
Take out trash	5 min./day	Jeremy
Weekly deep cleaning	8 hrs./week	Housekeeper
Weekly food shopping	1.5 hrs./week	Tracy and Mom
Gardening spring and summer	3 hrs./week	Jeremy

The Time It Takes to Delegate

At this point you may be wondering whether it's worth the time it takes to delegate. By the time you explain what needs to be done, you might as well have done the job yourself, right? While this thinking may apply to onetime tasks that will take you ten minutes or less to do, don't short-change yourself or the people in your life by hogging all the work.

Some things you can delegate and just not worry too much about the result. But for other tasks there are three stages of delegation that require a worthwhile investment of your time.

> **Present the job.** You've got to take some time to explain what needs to be done. This could take between five and fifteen minutes. Clear your head, describe the ultimate result you are looking for, and then allow your delegatee to be a little creative in how he or she gets there.
>
> **Be available for input and questions.** If your delegatee runs into snags, let him or her know where you'll be so he/she can approach you with questions. Again, consider the scale of the project in determining how much supervision is needed.
>
> **Review and evaluate the result.** If someone has invested time to do something for you, demonstrate respect for his or her contribution by reviewing the work, providing feedback, and expressing your gratitude.

Does it take time to delegate? Yes! Is it worth the effort? You bet. It involves other people in your life and frees you to make time for what's most important. That said, delegating is one of the most psychologically loaded of the time-management skills. If you are still having trouble delegating, read chapter 12, "Purge."

Once you've applied the WADE Formula to your pileup of

to-dos, you should feel more in control, even if there's still a lot of paper cluttering up your life. Never fear! The next chapter, "Where Paper Meets Time," will help you work through those piles of paper and prepare you for the bigger time-management issues to come.

5

WHERE PAPER MEETS TIME

Here's a little-known secret: Paper clutter is more often a symptom of poor time management than poor organizing skills.

Think about the areas in your home or office where paper has taken over:

- **Your desk at the office.** What's there? Unopened mail, trade journals, memos, messages, papers waiting to be filed, and projects you can't get on top of.
- **Your kitchen countertop.** What's there? Mail, catalogs, calendars, invitations to upcoming events, and reading material you haven't had time to go through or decide on.
- **Your briefcase.** What's there? Projects and reading material you've been carting back and forth between home and the office for weeks, with every intention of working on. You just never seem get to it.

Every year the U.S. Postal Service delivers more than 200 billion pieces of mail—and an estimated 30 billion e-mail messages bounce around the Internet every single day. *The Wall Street Journal* reported that U.S. executives waste an average of six weeks per year looking for items in cluttered desks and files—that works out to be about an hour a day.

The main problem with the constant flow of mail and information is the sheer volume. Once you fall behind, it's almost impossible to catch up. One overwhelmed client accumulated eighty banker's boxes' worth of unopened mail! She never felt there was enough time to get through it all, so she saved it, and saved it, until she had to install shelves in her garage to hold all the boxes. She couldn't imagine when she'd have time to deal with such an overwhelming project! Who could? The key to avoiding those suffocating and depressing pile-ups is to be aggressive.

In this quick-start chapter, you'll learn a three-step program to get on top of the time backlog represented by the piles of paper in your life. The added bonus of digging through this backlog is the energy you will gain from your newly clean desk and countertops, and the time you will save by not having to search for missing information in messy piles and files. Here's the plan:

Step #1—Assess the backlog.
Step #2—Weed it down.
Step #3—Stay ahead of the game.

The first two steps take about an hour each; the last varies from person to person. You may need to invest a few hours to get on top of your backlog, but when you are done, you'll regain an hour of time every day, not to mention the spring you'll have in your step.

STEP #1: ASSESS THE BACKLOG

SUPPLIES NEEDED: Post-its, pen.
What do you think is in those piles on your desk? The average ratio of any desktop or counter pileup is one-third things to do, two-thirds things to file or toss. Find out your ratio by first doing a quick sort of all the papers into three piles: to do, to file, to toss.

Avoid using this as a catch-up session. Don't stop to actually "do" any of the tasks you discover, or even throw anything out yet. This process is simply to sort and see what you have. If you allow yourself to get sidetracked by making a phone call, reading an interesting article, or filling out a registration form as you unearth it, you'll never get through the stacks and won't gather the information you need.

When you are finished sorting, assess your ratio. How much is each?

_____ percent to do

_____ percent to file

_____ percent to toss

Add Up Your To-Dos

Now take your pile of to-dos to see how many hours of work have accumulated. One by one, lift each item from the pile, and ask yourself three questions:

1. What is this document?
2. What is the next action I need to take on it? (Read? Fill out? Decide? Call?)
3. How long will that take me to do?

Notate the action and time estimate on a Post-it Note (e.g., fill out warranty card—fifteen minutes, write thank-you note—twenty minutes, track down address—ten minutes) and stick it to the paper.

When you're done assessing each piece of paper, take out a calculator and total the time estimates you put on the Post-its to see how much work is piled up. You may be surprised, but don't be afraid. Once you have a realistic estimate of the work waiting for you, you'll be inspired to let some of it go, or improve your delegation skills.

GETTING REAL

Donna—Paper Piles at Home

"Help!!!! Paper has taken over my life!" cried Donna. "You've got to help me organize my home office. There's no place for me to even sit."

During my initial meeting with Donna, we toured her office and, indeed, papers threatened to tumble off every available flat surface. Not just small piles, towers. Sliding into one another. Stacks of magazines and newspapers around her chair gave it a ceremonial air. We dissected the contents of the piles and discovered the usual combination of mail, catalogs, calendars, invitations to upcoming events, insurance forms, bills to pay, pending projects, memos, messages, requests for donations, magazines, books, and reminders to call about household repairs.

The problem wasn't the clutter but her time-management skills. We could certainly find a more attractive way to store her papers, but until she found time to take care of all the tasks in front of her, the clutter would never disappear.

"If I had just three uninterrupted hours, I could get on top of this backlog," Donna sighed, explaining that as a working mom she never had time to do paperwork at home.

"Let's see," I suggested. Paper by paper, we assigned a time value. In the end, it turned out to be nine and a half hours' worth of to-dos. Donna was shocked—she'd grossly underestimated! And she thought all she needed was a few extra file drawers.

Is the quantity of your backlog more or less than you thought? Reexamine your time estimates. Are you being realistic, or reverting to the "That'll take me two seconds" mentality. (See chapter 3 for a primer in making accurate time estimations.)

Now ask yourself if this buildup is typical for you. Are the piles on your desk the standard quantity that builds up over time? Or did something change in your life or job that has caused you to fall behind? Maybe, as you're weeding through the piles, you'll realize that your workload has changed in recent months.

If you are like most people, you've probably discovered that you have much more to do than you can possibly accomplish. Your next step is to reduce the backlog—and your stress level along with it.

STEP #2: WEED IT DOWN

SUPPLIES NEEDED: Planner, pen, trash bags.

Apply the Four Ds

How can you get yourself out from underneath the piles and the guilt? Use the four Ds (Delete, Delay, Diminish, Delegate) from chapter 4 to help you decide. Gather your courage to make some hard decisions. What can you let go of, wait even longer to do, give away, or just do a fast job on?

Try to reduce your backlog by at least two-thirds. If you found twelve hours' worth of work, pare it down to four. If you found six hours of work, get it down to two. Remember that many of those tasks were buried under the clutter for months, and if you hadn't done this exercise, they'd probably go undone for another six months anyway. Release the guilt, and the burden.

Using Your Planner to Eliminate Paper

You can easily live pile-free if you file everything, no matter what its stage of completion, and use your planner to keep track of what you need to do and when. Used to its full potential, a planner is a great paper-management tool. By recording critical info in your planner, you can trash the paper and keep your desk a clean, workable surface. (If you don't have a planner, jump to chapter 6, "Choosing the Right Planner for you.")

GETTING REAL

Fred, Mortgage Application

Fred had a mortgage application sitting on his desk for months. It was taking him forever to fill out because he had to gather information from his bank accounts, his accountant, and other investment files. Instead of keeping everything out, I suggested Fred note in his planner what day he wanted to continue working on the application (e.g., Saturday morning), then place the application in his "mortgage" file. When he gets to Saturday and sees "fill out mortgage application" on his planner page, he'd simply go to the mortgage file, pull out the half-written application, and move the task forward. If he needed to stop before the application is complete, again, he'd make a note in his planner as to when he will work on it again (maybe Sunday evening?), and then refile the application in the mortgage folder. Desktop cleared.

Continue to go through your to-do piles, and enter as much as you can in your planner, so you can either toss or file the paper. For example:

- **Meeting memo.** Record meeting date and time in your planner, including all the pertinent related information—attendees, location, phone number, directions, and important agenda points. Then toss the paper.

- **Notes from staff meeting.** Transfer any follow-up tasks you are responsible for into your planner (i.e., send new press kit materials to public relations director), then toss or file the notes from meeting.

- **Phone message/business card of person you met last week.** Record person's name and phone number in your planner on day you will call back, and toss the paper. If you need to update your address book or Rolodex or database, file the message slip in your Rolodex, or in a file named "update database." Schedule a time once a week or month to actually transfer that new info into your permanent system. Or, delegate the job to someone else.

- **Overstuffed file from recently completed project.** The reason it's on your desk is because you've been meaning to weed through it (tossing all the irrelevant stuff and saving the most important info), but you haven't had the time or energy to do it. File as is, and schedule a day in your planner to weed one drawer a month. Release your perfectionism on this one.

- **Brochure to upcoming conference you may or may not attend.** Record "decide on such and such conference" in your planner two days before the registration deadline, and *pencil* in the actual conference dates. The pencil indicates it's a tentative schedule item. File brochure in your association file.

- **Thirty-five business cards from conference you attended two years ago.** Do you remember who those people are anymore? If you do, file cards in the association file, and simply review them before next year's conference. Or, delegate the job of entering the contacts into your database. Try CardScan software to make quick work of it.

- **Baby announcement.** Write newborn's name and birth date on your calendar, and put "Buy baby Max a gift" on your Saturday to-do list. Note: If the announcement is over nine months old, jump ahead three months to the baby's birthday, and plan to send a first-birthday gift instead. Toss the announcement.

- **Coupon/e-mail promotion for free latte at your local bookstore.** Store in your wallet—conveniently placed where you'll need it. What good will it do sitting on your desk?
- **Subscription renewal card for magazine.** If you are ready to renew, fill it out immediately and mail. If not, toss it. Don't worry, they'll send you another one.

Toss Whatever You Can

Now, turn your attention to the pile of items to toss. Get a shredder, if you don't have one, and get caught up in the feeding frenzy of eliminating the stacks of unnecessary paper. There is little more satisfying than the sound of the shredder and watching surfaces reemerge on your desk.

Toss the following items without even thinking twice!

- **Junk mail.** If you aren't ready to make a purchase immediately, toss it. They'll send you another solicitation within a few weeks!
- **Brochures/catalogs you never refer to.** Keep the source (in your Rolodex or database), and toss the paper. Call the company to make sure you're on their list, so you'll always get their current catalog.
- **Magazines over three months old.**
- **Newspapers older than one week.**
- **Articles or clippings** you haven't referred back to in two years or more, or that contain information confirming what you already know.
- **Early drafts of letters and research material.** Save yourself the aggravation, and only keep the final version.
- **Duplicate printouts of documents** (if original is on the computer).

- **Expired invitations, coupons, warranties, and service contracts.**
- **Instructions and warranties** for items you no longer own.
- **Mangled, used, torn file folders.** Investing in new, clean folders will make your system shine.
- **Recipes you clipped, but never used.**
- **Old greeting cards** (with a few rare sentimental exceptions).
- **Road maps you haven't used in five years.**

Of course, these decisions might not be easy—you're probably holding on to paper and information because you're afraid to throw it away, or just don't know what else to do with it.

Ask these ten questions of every item you have trouble deciding on. If you answer yes to any of the following questions, it's fair to keep it. If no, let it go.

To Keep or to Toss—The Ten Questions

1. Are there tax/legal reasons to keep it?
2. Do I refer often to this piece of paper?
3. Will it help me complete a project I am working on right now?
4. Do I have time to do anything with this piece of paper?
5. Does it tie in with the core activities of my job?
6. Do I trust that the information is up to date?
7. Does it represent a viable business opportunity?
8. Will it help me make money?
9. Would my work suffer if I didn't have it?
10. If I ever needed it again, could I easily get it from someone else?—If someone else has the original, and you can get another copy, let your version go.

STEP #3: STAY AHEAD OF THE GAME

Reduce Your Reading Pile

We are all information junkies, but with more than 80,000 magazines in circulation, 100,000-plus books published in the United States alone, and literally millions of Web sites, there's no way to get to it all.

In reality, there isn't more information out there; there are just more versions of it—the same topics are reworked and reworded in dozens of newspapers, news magazines, and Web sites. Be selective. Instead of reading five magazines each month, pick your favorite two or three. If you receive publications you consistently don't have time to read, cancel your subscription. The sight of unread magazines or journals you'd like to read but don't have time to creates clutter and can make you feel guilty or overwhelmed.

If your job requires you to read several papers each day (to stay abreast of your industry, or give you fodder for projects), consider getting help from clipping services—they can give you the major headlines of the day (from every paper you read), but you can choose which articles to read closely and which ones to just skim. Alternatively, find a Web site that covers your industry and posts the "must reads" from each day. (*ABC News'* "The Note" is a great example for those interested in politics.)

And don't worry, any truly newsworthy information will eventually find its way to you—through a friend at a cocktail party, on a news program, or on the radio. Once you've heard the basics of the story, you can search online for more details, but only if you want to.

Speed Reading

Abby Marks-Beale is a reading specialist whose livelihood is based on helping people reduce their reading piles and get through the reading they do want to do, faster. For more innovative, speed-reading techniques like those below, see Abby's Web site, www. readmorefaster.com, or read her book *Ten Days to Faster Reading* (Warner Books, 2001).

• Do you frequently go back over material you already read? According to Abby, if you constantly flick your eyes back to a word or words you read already, you could be giving into *passive regression,* a habit that wastes your time, tires your eyes, and doesn't always ensure good comprehension! Try placing a blank 3 × 5 white card ON TOP of the words covering the text you already read, leaving exposed the words yet to read. This will force you to push your eyes down the page and help you resist the urge to reread unnecessarily. Focusing only on the words you are reading enhances your concentration, builds comprehension, keeps your eyes moving forward, and helps you keep your place.

• Abby says you *don't* need to read every word to understand—in fact, she says it's a serious waste of time! By using your peripheral vision, you can learn how to read more in less time by using key words, or reading in thought groups. Read the first sentences of paragraphs (on nonfiction, factual material only) to quickly find the paragraphs you want to spend your time on, and skip the rest. The key to effective skipping is in choosing what you read, not what you leave out. Overcome your fear of missing material. There is more than enough reading material to last a lifetime. Your job is to q-u-i-c-k-l-y find what is most valuable to you.

GETTING REAL

Tackling the Sunday Paper

Did you know that a daily edition of a big-city newspaper contains approximately the same number of words as a typical novel? And the Sunday edition contains the same number of words as four to six novels? No wonder you may feel overwhelmed by an entire Sunday newspaper! Use these tips to make it through, fast!

1. **Get rid of the clutter:** Start your process by getting rid of the unwanted circulars and sections that you don't need or want to spend your time on. They get in your way and distract you. Abby immediately removes the Automotive section (unless she is looking to buy a car) and Sports (she barely knows the difference between a goal and a homerun!).

2. **Set it up for faster reading:** Lay the newspaper flat out on a table with all the sections neatly underneath.

3. **Organize the sections based on your interests:** Looking at the cover page of each section, decide which ones intrigue you the most, and prioritize them accordingly. This way, if you run out of time, you have read the sections of most value to you.

4. **Skim the headlines:** Look for articles of interest. Disregard those you have no interest in.

5. **Read the first few paragraphs:** Most newspaper articles are written in an A-frame style; the most important, new information is up front, then the other, unimportant or older news details follow.

6. **Continue reading if you want more:** If not, don't! And for those who know speed-reading techniques, use them to get through the text faster.

Information provided by Abby Marks-Beale. www.readmore faster.com

Improve Your Filing System

If you don't currently have a filing system that works for you (which is why all those papers were out in the first place!), it is worth the time to figure out what is wrong and to fix it.

With a bad filing system, you'll waste an enormous amount of time looking for misplaced information and redoing work or research because you can't find your originals. When your files are organized and you can find what you need when you need it, it feels fabulous. You don't waste time hunting for things and you can hit the ground running every day. Your space will energize and support, instead of intimidating and overwhelming, and you'll waste less time procrastinating.

Let's figure out what's wrong with your system and what you can do to make it easier to find and file the information you deem important. These are the most common mistakes people make in setting up their files:

1. **Files are located too far from the workstation.** If you can't file or retrieve documents without getting out of your chair, your file storage is inconvenient.
   Solution: Move active files within an arm's reach of your work surface. Then you can file as you go, and don't need to set aside a separate time to file. If you must file at a location far from your work area, indicate which file each paper belongs in (with a small Post-it in the corner) so that by the time you are filing, you don't have to reread papers to remember where they belong. Create a To File box, and schedule time—once per day or week, to file.
2. **Filing system is too complicated.** You worry that if you put something away, you might never find it. If you have five

hundred folders, with one piece of paper in each, this might be your problem.

Solution: File by topic (Mortgage, Client Jones, Wedding Plans) rather than urgency (urgency changes, but topic remains consistent). Use "Out Guides" to make refiling easier. For help designing a simple, logical system that offers visual cues for quick and easy retrieval of any item, see *Organizing from the Inside Out* (Henry Holt/Owl Books, 2004).

3. **Filing is boring.** OK, yes, it can be. There are a zillion more interesting, enjoyable, and profitable ways to spend your time—like hanging out with friends, writing a new business proposal, or reading the paper.

   Solution: Make it more fun, by adding your own personal pizzazz. See the tips below to learn about appealing to your aesthetics.

Add some visual flair to your system to motivate yourself to file every day, and make the files look interesting, so you are inspired to use them.

- **Color-code.** Plain manila folders are blah! Add some spunk to your system with colored folders. Divide your files into three to five categories (e.g., financial, vital records, lifestyle, home improvement) and assign each category a different rich color (e.g., financial files might be green—for money, lifestyle in yellow—for fun). Think beyond the primary colors for richer hues, like burgundy, lavender, pumpkin, and gold.

- **Place colored folders in standard green hanging files.** The dark background makes the colored folders pop—and when you remove a file to work with it, the hanging folder stays in the drawer, conveniently marking its place. When you open the drawer it's easy to see what files are missing and exactly where you should return files.

- **Use quality folders.** Invest in two-ply top folders for just a few pennies extra per folder. They have reinforced edges, which make them much more durable than single-ply folders. They also won't dog-ear or sag in the file drawer, lending the appropriate dignity to the information you are storing in them.
- **Try straight-line filing.** Most of us were taught to alternate file tab positions, left, center, right, left, center, right. There are two problems with this approach: (1) the minute you delete or add a file, you break the pattern and start worrying about what folders are hiding behind others; and (2) scanning back and forth between titles makes many people anxious—a sort of horizontal vertigo effect. Straight-line filing (with all the tabs lined up in the same position, one behind the other) is much easier on the eye. You can add or delete files at any time, without worrying about ruining your pattern.
- **Use tab coding.** Once you have established a pattern of straight-line filing, you can alter tab position to communicate important information to yourself. For example, in your travel files, you could keep completed trips in left-tab folders (retaining all the travel info you'd ever want to refer back to) and possible trips in right-tab folders (containing research you've done on packages, hotels, and places to see)—all arranged alphabetically by destination. When a possible trip becomes a reality, you can simply turn the folder inside out, so it has a left-tab position.
- **Label clearly.** A label produced on a label maker speaks with far more authority than a barely legible chicken-scratched title in pencil. As a result, you tend to honor the system you've set up and place things in their proper folders. Take the time to create beautiful labels, either electronically or by handwriting in very neat, block letters with a medium-width marker, and you will see the difference it makes. White labels with bold black lettering are easiest to read.

Remember, files are for retrieval, not storage. We keep paper so we can access it, not just hide it away. Imagine how satisfying it is to look for your Automobile file and find a copy of your registration card!

Set Aside Daily Time to Process Paperwork

We all know that being disorganized wastes time. If you can stay a few steps ahead of the curve, you'll be able to maintain your system. The biggest mistake people make is just checking their incoming paperwork and saving it as "new." Use the following strategies to stem the tide and prevent another backlog.

- **Have a mail station.** Open mail near your filing system (not on the train, or at the doctor's office), so you can file the information you want to save, instantly. Stand over a trash can while opening the mail and feed it generously. Then, sort whatever remains into baskets by person, or category (bills, invitations, magazines).
- **Schedule a daily time to process mail.** It's usually better to process mail daily, as it comes in, rather than allowing it to accumulate—there's just something about anything old that makes it harder to look through! So, is it fifteen minutes per day? thirty minutes, an hour? Go through your mail at a peak-energy time, so you'll be able to make decisions more quickly.
- **Get and stay off lists.** It takes some work, but it's well worth the effort. Remove your name from many national mailing lists with the Direct Marketing Association's Mail Preference Service (www.dmaconsumers.org). Additional opt-out sources can be found at The Center for Democracy and Technology, which even generates the letters for you! (http://opt-out.cdt.org/submit.shtml). Avoid getting on lists in the first place, by writing "do not sell, rent or trade my name" when filling out war-

ranties, making donations, or placing catalog orders. Complaints about companies who ignore your removal requests can be filed with the Consumer Protection Association of America (www. consumerpro.com).

- **Don't put projects into your briefcase, without scheduling when you are going to work on them.** At the end of your workday or workweek, don't shove projects or reading into your bag, hoping to do it if you happen to have a little free time. *There is no such thing as free time.* Only bring work or reading home if you have scheduled a specific time to do it! Same rule applies to projects and folders you bring on trips—only bring them if you know when you're going to do them.

- **Most important, be decisive.** Get out of the habit of "just checking"—looking at what's come in, deciding you aren't ready to deal with it, and putting it back in your inbox. Once you open a piece of mail or new document, move it forward in some way by either taking action on it, tossing it, or filing it immediately. Need to make a phone call or renew a subscription? Do it now. Have to consult your spouse on an invitation? Place it in a separate "discuss with Jim" folder. Then set aside time to talk.

NOTE: If you live by the "out of sight, out of mind" mentality, make sure the visual reminders you use are really working for you. How do you know? If the content of your to-do pile changes every day because you remember to do things, then your system is OK.

But if you are like most people, before long your visual-reminder system becomes visual Muzak, which you eventually tune out, ignoring everything except the top piece of paper on each pile. If the piles are stagnant, the system isn't working for you and you need to create a new one.

GETTING REAL

Lonnie, HR Manager, Just Checking

Lonnie had always wrestled with her in-box. A towering pile of mail, to-dos, notes, finished projects, and reading material, she had developed the bad habit of cherry-picking the most important tasks and just leaving the rest as new.

What was really left in the box were what she called her Misery Tasks—things she dreaded taking care of. Once a month she devoted a day to clearing it out. The problem with keeping them in her in-box was that they got mixed up with all the truly new material. What's worse, her towering in-box became an intimidating distraction—taunting her every day from the corner of her eye. When she finally resigned herself to sort through it all, it would eat up half a day.

To make her space more welcoming and easier to work in, we devised a "Misery Task Basket" and placed it underneath her desk. As she sorted new material from her in-box, anything she wanted to postpone now got tossed into the Misery Basket under her desk. This kept her in-box a pure location, filled with all genuinely new and urgent items.

Lonnie scheduled one day each month to work on all the tasks that had accumulated in her Misery Basket—which is what she had been doing all along, except with the new system, she didn't need to think about those dreaded tasks until her scheduled day. On her Misery Basket Days, she gave fair warning to her coworkers on the mood she'd be in and, to ease the blow, encouraged them to bring her cookies!

When you are overwhelmed with the feeling that there is too much to do, and not enough time, taking control of your paper piles is one of the most effective solutions.

This quick-start program just helped you take control and gain an hour back every day. Now let's put it to good use! Having gotten out from under, let's step back from the details and begin designing your schedule and your life, from the inside out.

PART III
ANALYZE
Tuning In to Who You Are

6

CHOOSING THE RIGHT PLANNER FOR YOU

Everyone needs a planner. Whether your life is superbusy or calm, whether you have a good memory or not, and whether you are in school, working, a business owner, retired, or a socialite, everyone needs some sort of calendar-based tool to manage his or her life. But with the thousands of choices on the market, the challenge is finding the right one for you.   .

Having the wrong planner can be just as frustrating as having none at all. An oversized, leather-bound paper planner is a total mismatch for the regional sales rep already weighed down with catalogs, samples, and other bulky materials she has to lug with her to every meeting. Likewise, a sleek electronic organizer may be your idea of the perfect Father's Day gift, but your retired techno-phobe dad has other ideas. Your planner becomes an extension of yourself. To keep track of all you have to do—to-dos, appointments, meetings, activities—you need the time-management tool that complements who you are.

If you have tried using a planner in the past but abandoned it because it didn't work for you, chances are you made one of these three common mistakes:

1. You didn't pick a planner that was right for you.
2. You didn't take time to master its features and make it yours.
3. You didn't make it the one and only place to record your appointments and to-dos, so you never came to rely on it.

GETTING REAL

Elise, Finding the Right Planner

Elise's days were out of control. She'd tried different planners, but with no success. First, there was the magnetic refrigerator calendar. That lasted a few weeks until the dog got hold of the magnets and started using them as chew toys.

Then she tried a paper planner she spotted in the supermarket's stationery section. She loved the designated sections for menus, shopping, bill paying, and life goals. But the pages were undated. She filled in the first month and was into mid-February when she realized she had mislabeled one day, which threw her entire schedule off. Exasperated, she dumped the thing in the garbage.

After the "date-it-yourself" fiasco, her husband came to the rescue (or so he thought) with a brand-new, late-model PalmPilot. Surely, that was the answer—it did everything for you. All she had to do was enter the information. Nope. Keying in to-dos drove Elise crazy, and she didn't like the way it presented time—she never felt like she could actually get a grip on her schedule. Plus, it was so small (and expensive) that she didn't dare take it out of the house for fear of losing it.

When Elise called me for help, she was using an array of Post-it Notes, napkins, scraps of paper, a whiteboard, and a few different notebooks placed strategically (in the computer room, on her nightstand, in the kitchen) to track her to-dos. She lived in constant fear of double-booking, missing appointments, and disappointing friends. One Saturday, she inadvertently agreed to five conflicting activities and ended up missing three.

To me the problem was clear. Elise hadn't been using the right planner.

Elise was a visual person, so I prescribed a very simple paper planner with a monthly overview and one-page-per-day close-up.

At first Elise resisted writing everything in one place, not just appointments, but also calls, errands, and chores. But as invitations and obligations came up, she dutifully asked herself how long each would take her, determined when she would do it, and then blocked out time for it in her planner.

Three weeks later Elise was giddy over the results. "It's amazing! I write everything down in my planner and it feels like I have triple the amount of free time! Knowing I'm on top of everything allows me to live more fully in the moment. I took the kids to the zoo last week for two hours—and I enjoyed every minute! Most important, it's so much easier to say no. I used to say yes to everything. Now, when somebody asks me if I can do something, I flip through my planner and can see in black and white whether I have time or not."

No matter which planner you use, it's essential that you apply the "select one" rule: making it the one and only place where you record all your activities, appointments, and things to do.

What about having one for work and one for your personal life? Most people don't keep work and personal life completely and totally separate—they make a few personal calls at work and do some work from home, too. The point is, you have one life; you need one planner. With everything in one place, you can really keep an eye on your balance.

There are three main choices you need to make in selecting a planner.

Choice #1—Paper or Electronic. No matter what the technological whizzes come up with, some people do better with paper-based planners, while others thrive on the latest digital devices. Crossing over to a platform that is a bad fit usually results in failure. Once you figure out which world you belong in, the rest of the choices are easier.

Choice # 2—Stationary or Portable. If you do all your planning and implementing from one location (e.g., your computer at work, or your desk at home), you can utilize a stationary planner, such as a desktop, wall, or computer calendar program. If you're mobile and make plans and appointments while out and about, you'll need a portable system, whether paper or electronic. You'll be looking for the smallest feasible planner that can contain all the information you need with you while on the road.

Choice #3—Brand, Features. Once you've narrowed your choices, you can pick between brands and special features, decisions that are based solely on your own circumstances and sense of aesthetics.

Start by looking at your natural preferences.

VISUAL/TACTILE VS. LINEAR DIGITAL

Visual/Tactile

If you are a visual/tactile person, you belong on a paper-based system. How do you know if you are visual/tactile? Here are some clues that that description fits you:

- You tend to remember where on a page you wrote things down. ("The phone number is on the lower right-hand corner of the page, in green ink.")
- Your thinking flows most easily when writing things out, pen on paper.
- The act of physically writing things out helps you remember them.
- You like to flip back and forth between pages in your planner in order to get events in perspective (like Elise, who needed to see the whole view to really understand what was going on).
- You write to-do lists in terms of association or groupings (things to buy, things to write, calls to make) rather than in terms of sequence, priority, and chronology.
- You enjoy storing your old notebooks to pore over years later.
- In general, you find computer technology cumbersome and time-consuming.

Linear/Digital

Linear/digital people do very well on an electronic platform. Clues that you are linear/digital rather than visual/tactile are:

- Your thinking flows easily from fingers to keyboard.
- You are more likely to do a word search for a name or number than try to remember where you wrote a piece of information.
- You can look at one screen representing a day, or a week, and get events in perspective.
- You generally remember appointments by date, days of the month, times of the day. ("The concert is on Tuesday, two days after my husband's birthday on Sunday the twenty-sixth.")
- You think in terms of sequence, priority, and chronology, rather than in terms of association or groupings.

- You don't feel the need to look back at what you've done in the past few days to plan out what to do today and later in the week; you mentally carry over your to-do list from day to day.
- You feel right at home with computers or electronics.

PAPER-BASED OPTIONS

Stationary Planners

Wall or desk calendars. There are two circumstances in which a desk or a wall calendar could function as an important component of your time-management system.

1. If you work from one place all the time and your schedule is straightforward, you can use a stand-alone calendar to successfully manage your time. One home-based business owner I know records his appointments on his desk calendar. Each morning, he checks the calendar and transfers his appointments for the day (including address and phone numbers), along with his to-do list, on an index card. He then tucks the index card in his pocket and heads out. Since his schedule is relatively uncomplicated, this system is sufficient for his needs.

GETTING REAL
Linda, the Mobile To-Do System

Linda a stay-at-home mom I worked with wanted to use a large desk planner but maintain flexibility by plucking a few to-dos to cart around with her for the day (shown on page 123). We got her a large desk calendar with one week on a page. She wrote each of her to-dos on a small Post-it Note and conscientiously included at the bottom the time it would take and what type of task it was (Self, Family, etc.). Linda could lay out her to-dos at the bottom of the page and move them to specific days as she determined when she would tackle them. When she went out she grabbed that day's to-dos and placed them on a notepad in her bag. This system also gave her the flexibility to rearrange her plans based on her kids' constantly changing needs.

If Linda didn't get to a task, she could just transfer the sticky from her notepad to a future day or week on her desk calendar. Once she did complete a task, she found it extremely satisfying to crumple up the Post-it Note and throw it away.

2. You can use your wall calendar as a communication device. This works well in families, where each family member can keep track of everyone else's schedule at a glance. Appoint one person to be the keeper of the calendar; he or she will confirm tomorrow's appointments with everyone at the end of previous day.

Wall calendars, however, have two serious limitations as time-management systems. For one thing, they are not good for recording to-do lists. Remember, for every to-do, you must ask yourself *when* you are going to do it. Also, since you can't exactly carry your wall calendar around in your briefcase, you'll still need a portable planner. You also might run into trouble if you are recording appointments on both your desk calendar and in your planner, so elect one. In most cases you'll opt to use a portable planner because it's more convenient and efficient. These calendars are useful tools for displaying the date and the day of the week.

Portable Planners

Paper-based products vary in size, ranging from pocket-sized up to 8.5 by 11 inches. Some are spiral bound. Others feature three-ring binders so you can add and delete pages. Consider the size of your handwriting, how much you have to record, and the way you view time to help determine the ultimate size and page format of your planner.

Format Features and Brand (At-A-Glance, Day Runner, Day-Timer, Time Design, FranklinCovey, Filofax)

Whether you choose pocket size, classic, binder, or spiral, here are some basic features to look for:

1. Every planner must include a **monthly view** for appointments, holidays, and events.

2. Every planner must also have a **close-up view** for daily to-dos and details. Choose a format that accommodates the number of to-dos and the size of your handwriting.

> **Week on two pages:** easily accommodates four to five daily to-dos
>
> **One page per day:** six to ten daily to-dos
>
> **Two pages per day:** ten-plus daily to-dos and tracking other people's schedules

3. Extra features: Many planners provide sections to track everything from expenses to shopping lists, books to buy, directions to appointments, projects to do, phone numbers and addresses, birthdays, gift lists, and more. Choose the features you find useful, and toss or ignore the others.

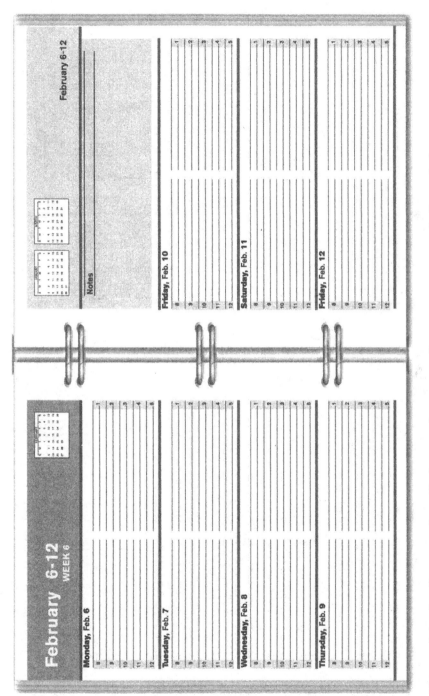

This week-in-view format works well when you have one to four items on your to-do list each day.

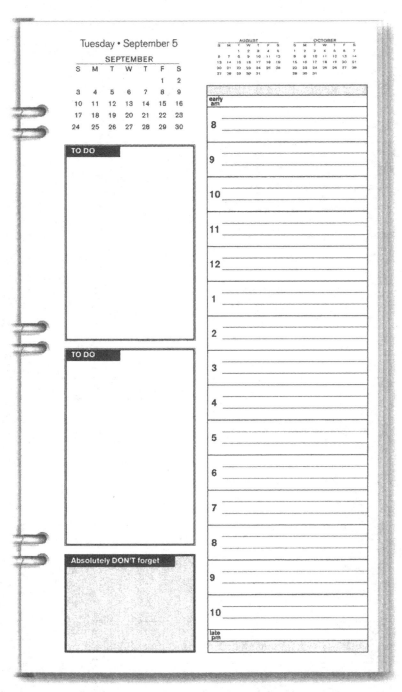

Tuesday • September 5

	SEPTEMBER					
S	M	T	W	T	F	S
					1	2
3	4	5	6	7	8	9
10	11	12	13	14	15	16
17	18	19	20	21	22	23
24	25	26	27	28	29	30

TO DO

TO DO

Absolutely DON'T forget

early am
8
9
10
11
12
1
2
3
4
5
6
7
8
9
10
late pm

The **one-page-per-day** format is better when you have ten to twelve items on your to-do list each day.

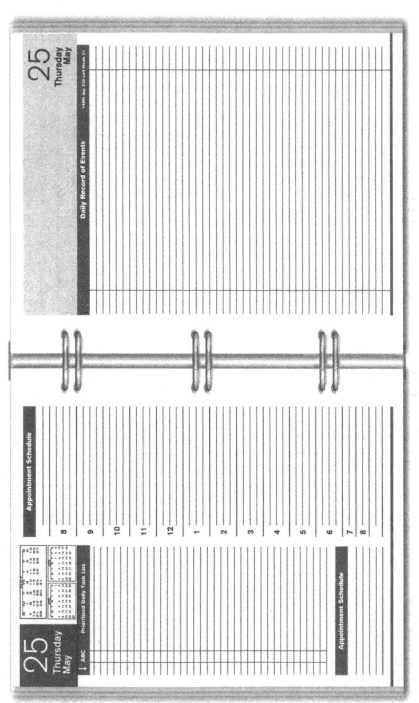

The **two-page-per-day** format works best when you have twelve or more items on your to-do list each day; plus you want to include additional information such as expense records, assistant's to-do list, etc.

Appointment Schedule

8	Book Chapters 2, 3
9	meet w/Karyn
10	Phone calls
11	Review makeover cards. Proof mag.
12	
1	Open, as needed
2	
3	Interview t.M.
4	Calls
5	Family Time
6	
7	
8	

Prioritized Daily Task List — ABC

Diane's to-dos

Appointment Schedule
Travel Arrangements L.A.
Synchronize Act
Pack stuff ?, Barn
FedEx guidelines
Type talking points for speech

Daily Record of Events

later day 2 to-Let week 21

Do: Proofread copy P Mag
Chapters 2,3
Order new computer
Review makeover candidates
J. Lillian — e-mail the plan

Calls: Angie K.
Patti F.
Kristy N.
Michael A. — Strategic plan
B. Jones — new space
N. Hirsch — Publicity plan
J. Welch — PBS

Suzanne M. Plan MSNBC speech

Two-page-per-day paper format allows for visual groupings of types of tasks.

If you have a lot of information to record, but don't want to carry around something bulky, get a planner with a smaller ring circumference, and carry around only a month's worth of sheets at a time.

When it comes to paper planners, the brand is largely a matter of aesthetics. Go to a well-stocked office-supply store, and actually handle the organizers you are considering. Do you like the way the planner looks and feels? Does it present time in a way that makes sense to you and fits the way you work? Some planners are designed more for linear types who think in terms of chronological lists; others are better suited for nonlinear thinkers who naturally group notes by category on a page. If you are wavering, follow your gut, and choose the one you were drawn to first.

SUMMING UP

Paper-Based Planners

The great thing about paper planners is you don't have to worry about batteries or electricity, and entering information is faster than navigating an electronic device. The one big hangup? If you lose your planner you're in big trouble—there's no backup!

Pros	Cons
• Easy to set up, no installation	• It can't do searches
• Writing feels natural	• Potentially bulky and heavy
• It doesn't need batteries	• Difficult to back up infor-
• You can flip back and forth	mation
between pages for an overview	• Other people can't access
• You can store old planner	schedule
pages for easy reference	

ELECTRONIC OPTIONS

Stationary Computer Programs

If you are at your desk most of the day, you can get a lot out of software calendar programs. A contact manager (such as Outlook, Act!, or Goldmine) is primarily a database program that helps you focus on everything you need to do for your clients (these work especially well for salespeople), but a personal information manager (PIM), such as Now Update, and Contact, is really designed to manage yourself—your appointments or to-dos. For the purposes of the rest of this chapter, we'll be talking about PIMs because they have a broader application.

In a company setting, where many people need access to your schedule, a network-enabled calendar is extremely efficient. Your assistant can update your schedule. Your colleagues can see at a glance when you are booked, which makes it easier to arrange meetings.

If you use the software program on your desktop as your sole time-management tool, and are mobile, print out pages and carry them with you. When you're out of the office, you have to record new appointments on paper and enter them into the computer when you get back to your desk. This method can be cumbersome and is accident-prone, so I don't recommend it. But, if you are disciplined enough to input the information as soon as you get back to your computer, or if you have an assistant who can enter the data for you, it might work.

Portable Electronic Systems

PDAs. PDA (Personal Digital Assistant) technology is improving at a rapid pace. Almost all PDAs now come with wireless Internet capability, and many brands combine phones, PDAs, cameras, and e-mail devices into one unit. Models from PalmPilot, like the simple m130 and the Treo 600 (which is a four-in-one device—phone, camera, PDA, and Web device), and Toshiba's PocketPC e335 are popular favorites. There are more choices than ever before, and there's no need to buy a PDA that has bells and whistles you don't need. A simple electronic organizer will organize your time, to-do lists, and contact information very well. If you spend a lot of time on the road or are out in the field regularly, advanced features that make your life easier might be well worth the cost.

Competition to make the smallest and the lightest product is fierce. But there *is* such a thing as too small! If you can't read the display without squinting, or if the screen is too tiny to accommodate your data, you will not be able to enjoy your electronic organizer's other features, no matter how wonderful they are.

The synch feature on all these devices makes it easy to enter appointments, contacts, and to-dos on your desktop (instead of entering them directly into your PDA, which can be cumbersome). Of course, technology has its disadvantages, too. Namely, using PDAs takes more time than glancing at or writing an entry on a page of a paper planner. It also takes longer to learn how to use PDAs, so many eager buyers end up using them simply as electronic address books.

Marrying Paper and Electronic

If you love your PDA for its size and features, but have never been able to use it to manage your to-dos, try marrying "paper to palm" by placing a dated notebook the size of your carrying case (write in the dates by hand, if need be) on the left-hand side of the case, next to your PDA. Now you'll have the convenience and power of your Palm, and the speed of pen-to-paper for quickly jotting down to-dos.

This month-view printout from a PalmPilot allowed me to schedule the repeated task of writing from 8 a.m. to 12 p.m. every day with just one entry.

May

Monday	Tuesday	Wednesday	Thursday	Friday	Saturday	Sunday
1 9–1p Northwest #504–9:10AM–12:5... 4–5p Wendy P. –workingwoman	**2** 8–12p Writing TMIO 1–2p IMRA Handouts!!!	**3** 8–12p Writing TMIO 10–11p JFK to LAX	**4** 9–2p Writing TMIO 4–11p NAPO Convention	**5** 1–2p MSNBC–The Homepage 10–6p Rehearsal PBS special	**6** 8–12p Writing TMIO 4–11 NAPO Convention 10–6p Rehearsal PBS special	**7** 8–12p Writing TMIO 4–11p NAPO Convention 9–5p Taping PBS special 7p NW flight 1610 to Nashville
8 8–9a IMRA Set Up 10–11a IMRA Convention in Nashville 2–6p Writing TMIO 8–9p Fly back to LGA	**9** 8–12p Writing TMIO	**10** 8–12p Writing TMIO	**11** 8–12p Writing TMIO	**12** 8–12p Writing TMIO 1–2p MSNBC–The Home Page 5:15–6:30p Linda	**13** 8–12p Writing TMIO	**14** 8–12p Writing TMIO
15 8–12p Writing TMIO	**16** 8–12p Writing TMIO 10–4p Accountant	**17** 8–12p Writing TMIO	**18** 8–12p Writing TMIO	**19** 8–12p Writing TMIO 1–2p MSNBC–The Home Page	**20** 8–12p Writing TMIO	**21** 8–12p Writing TMIO

Monday	Tuesday	Wednesday	Thursday	Friday	Saturday	Sunday
22 8–12p Writing TMIO	**23** 8–12p Writing TMIO 10:15–11p Linda	**24** 8–12p Writing TMIO	**25** 8–12p Writing TMIO –6p Seminar Center	**26** 8–12p Writing TMIO 1–5p Do–eMail Terry regarding speech title Research statistics Sign books for IMRA folks Pay bills CALLS—more	**27** 8–12p Writing TMIO	**28** 8–12p Writing TMIO
29 8–12p Writing TMIO	**30** 8–12p Writing TMIO	**31** 8–12p Writing TMIO	**1**	**2**	**3**	**4**
5	**6**	**7**	**8**	**9**	**10**	**11**

Alternatively, if you prefer paper but must keep your schedule on your computer at work for networking purposes, print out your calendar and tuck it into your planner to carry around. Record changes on the printout while out of the office. Update your computer schedule first thing each morning.

FORMAT, FEATURES, AND BRAND

Computer programs almost always provide multiple views, so you don't have to choose, though you do want to establish some consistency in which formats you use regularly. What features do you really need? What will you be using it for? I recommended using a program that can visually indicate a block of time. For example, when you've recorded that 2 p.m.–to–5 p.m. appointment, does the program clearly block off the whole three hours with color or a pattern? Or does the appointment show up only on the 2 p.m. line?

For digital planners, consider whether the user interface presents time in a way that you can easily work with. Can you deal with having your to-do list on one screen and your appointment list on another?

You also need to consider whether the program is compatible with your hardware and operating system. If you're unsure, you may be able to download a trial version of the program under consideration and spend a little time working with it before you make an investment. Remember that while there is bound to be a learning curve, figuring out how to use an organizing program shouldn't be so complex that you lose huge amounts of time feeling disoriented and nonproductive. The big-name paper-based planners have corresponding software, so if you are thinking about transitioning from paper to electronic, look first at the brand that's already familiar and comfortable.

SUMMING UP

Digital Planners

Digital formats offer the ability to back up information. They also give other people access to your schedule and require less rewriting once key information is entered. Portable versions are featherweight.

Pros	Cons
• You can search for information by keyword, date	• It is hard to get a visual overview (one screen at a time)
• You can easily group and rearrange data	• Archival information is not as accessible
• It's easy to back up your information	• It's not as easy to reference
• The data are easy to network, so other people can access your schedule	• It's not as quick to access as paper
	• It is difficult for visual/tactile people to use

GOING LINEAR/DIGITAL WHEN YOU'RE VISUAL/TACTILE

Even if you're a visual/tactile person, you might want to make the journey to an electronic/digital system if other people need easy access to your agenda. Or your company might require you to use a computer-based system. If you have a lot of information to record in your planner, the weight and bulk of a paper-based system might be too much for you.

If you're a visual/tactile person and you are going to try to switch to a digital format, keep in mind that the changeover may not be easy and there may be a loss of productivity in the process. In making the transfer, it is better to make the technology adapt to you, rather than the other way around.

Look into tablet-based planners that allow you to write on the tablet with a pen or stylus, instantly converting your writing into digital format for storage and easy retrieval. Ask yourself what you like about your paper planner—how you use it and how you like to see your information—and then see if you can adapt your electronic program to work the way you think. You want to make sure this new system can accommodate the way you organize information.

TAKING OWNERSHIP OF YOUR PLANNER

No matter which planner you choose, you need to spend at least a week or two customizing your system. Read the manual, then feel free to get creative. Don't limit yourself to using it only in the way the planner company intended! Decide where you are going to record different types of information (e.g., appointments, addresses, to-do lists, expenses). You can ignore the times printed on the left, or write your notes in the section they allot to calls. If you have an electronic planner, you can usually alter the settings and options to suit your preference. Get familiar with the program's quirks and shortcuts.

Plug in your annual events—birthdays, anniversaries, checkups, and car maintenance—at the beginning of the year. (If you are using a computerized system, you can forward this information automatically into the next year.) Then create areas for any other

February
WEEK BEGINNING FEBRUARY 6

FEBRUARY

Monday, Feb. 6

8 _____ 1

9 _____ 2

10 _____ 3

Pick up supplies for barbecue

Discuss barbecue plans with Laura

11 _____ 4

30 min. errand

12 _____ 5

20 min. errand

20 min. errand

20 min. call

20 min. call

20 min. call

Tuesday, Feb. 6

20 min. call

8 _____ 1

10 min. call

10 min. call

9 _____ 2

5 min. call

10 _____ 3

11 _____ 4

Fill out application for kids' summer camp

12 _____ 5

20 min. paperwork

15 min. paperwork

15 min. paperwork

Wedne *15 min. paperwork*

8 _____ 1

15 min. paperwork

10 min. paperwork

9 _____ 2

5 min. paperwork

5 min. paperwork

Fix drip in kitchen faucet

10 _____ 3

30 min. fix it

11 _____ 4

15 min. fix it

12 _____ 5

If you like to be more flexible with your to-do list, write your to-dos on small Post-it Notes, cluster them, and move them around in your planner as desired.

information you'd like to record: family clothing sizes, room measurements, passwords, creative ideas.

Your planner becomes an extension of you. Be sure to record every phone call, every project, every appointment, and every task on your to-do list, bar none.

Writing in an attractive, legible hand is very grounding and calming. Not only does it make reading your list easier when it comes time to take action, slowing down forces you to think through each task and decide: Is this really worth doing?

Keep your planner visible and refer to it constantly. At the end of each day, schedule fifteen quiet minutes to review your to-do list and check off what you've accomplished. Reschedule unfinished tasks for another day, or delete them if it turns out they're just not that important.

As you embark on your quest, remember that no planner is absolutely perfect. You may find one that you love, adore, and come to depend on, but I have never met anyone whose planner didn't have a couple of irritating shortcomings. Pick a planner you really like, customize it to your heart's content, and then learn to live with its foibles. It will be a supportive, dependable friend for years to come, helping you achieve your goals and live your life to the fullest.

Now that you have a planner, let's track where your time goes.

7

UNDERSTANDING YOUR UNIQUE RELATIONSHIP TO TIME

"To thine own self be true."
—William Shakespeare

The next step in your journey to becoming a better time manager is to do an honest self-assessment. This evaluation will help you harness your strengths and will save you time by focusing your efforts on just those areas that need improvement. Perhaps most important, it helps you develop a deeper understanding of your unique relationship to time.

> I am such a procrastinator. I occupy my time with trivial matters and then rush in the final hours to do what's important. I want less stress and more pride in my life.
>
> *—Clive G.*

> I never get anywhere on time. I try to pack way too much in before going anywhere or I procrastinate prior to leaving. This creates a lot of pressure, yelling, and embarrassing situations for myself, and my kids.
>
> *—Trisha H.*

My days are extremely productive and well-organized. I don't waste a second. But, I really need to find a way to relax sometimes. It's hard for me to just get quiet and chill out.

—*Zoraida K.*

While everyone reading this book feels frustrated with the way he or she is currently managing time, your specific issues are highly individualized. By examining your unique time-management experience, you will learn a tremendous amount of valuable information about yourself.

Buried under the chaos and confusion of your days are clues about your individual strengths and weaknesses, personality style and preferences, what energizes you and what makes you happy. By tuning in to your individuality now, you begin the process of custom designing a time-management solution that truly matches who you are.

In exploring your relationship to time, we will examine three areas:

1. What's working and what's not
2. Your time management preferences
3. Your energy cycles and sources

You may be surprised what you discover!

WHAT'S WORKING?

No matter how out of control your life may seem, there are always some things that work for you in addition to the long list of things that do not. It is invaluable to start by looking at what works. First of all, it will boost your self-confidence, as you inevitably discover that you do possess some time-management skills, even if they are only "selectively applied" at the moment. When you've discovered these skills, you can begin to build on them in other areas of your life.

Identifying what's working will save you an enormous amount of time and energy because, clearly, there is no need to fix what isn't broken. It will also provide critical clues about what appeals to you—information that will help you fix all the areas that aren't working.

Think about what's working for you. Use the questionnaire below to help get you started. Think long and deep about these questions, and consider all the areas of your life—work, home, relationships, personal growth—when answering. You may want to type your answers on a computer or write them in a notebook so there's plenty of room for answers.

EXERCISE #1: WHAT'S WORKING?

Fill in as many answers to the following questions as you can think of:

No matter how busy I get, I always find time to _____.

My goals are well defined when it comes to_____.

I'm pretty clear on how long it takes me to _____.

I never procrastinate about _____.

I am never late for _____.

I enjoy exercising when _____.

I'm able to tackle difficult projects when _____.

I always build in transition time between_____.

It's easy for me to say no to _____.

Meeting deadlines is easiest for me when _____.

I am at my happiest when I am_____.

The things that I delegate easy are _____.

Sample answers:

No matter how busy I get, I always find time to read to my kids at night, clean out my fridge, see new clients, get the invoices out.

My goals are well defined when it comes to <u>my kids, my work, my marriage.</u>

I'm pretty clear on how long it takes me to <u>walk to work, get dressed in the morning, shave, cook dinner, go food shopping, write a proposal.</u>

I never procrastinate about <u>feeding the baby, gardening, paying the mortgage, eating dinner, writing in my journal.</u>

I am never late for <u>a flight, a dinner date, client appointments, the movies, doctors.</u>

I enjoy exercising when I <u>first wake up, am on vacation, am watching TV, have a workout buddy.</u>

I'm able to tackle difficult projects when <u>it's Monday morning, I have enough lead time, my kids are not around, it involves other people.</u>

I always build in transition time between <u>work and home, one creative task and another, working with numbers, playing with my kids.</u>

It's easy for me to say no to <u>requests for volunteering, my mother-in-law, unreasonable demands, working overtime.</u>

Meeting deadlines is easiest for me when <u>the deadline is set by someone else, I'm under pressure, there's money on the line, at work.</u>

I am at my happiest when I am <u>in my garden, brainstorming new ideas, dancing, surfing the Internet.</u>

The things that I delegate easily are <u>the laundry, data entry, taking out the trash, copyediting, legal work.</u>

Now, look over your answers and see what you can learn about yourself. Ask yourself why these particular things are working. Are you getting to certain tasks because you enjoy them so much? Or because you are very skilled at them? Are you responding to outside pressures ("If I don't do it, I'll get fired, so I always get it done") or self-imposed ones ("If I don't do this, I won't be happy with myself")? Does it have to do with the time of day that you choose to do them, or the amount of time each one takes? Are you better at doing solitary tasks than collaborative ones? Ask yourself what makes these things work. Even if some of the areas that are under control in your life seem trivial, they can help you figure out how to fix other, bigger problems.

GETTING REAL

Jane, Lawyer

Jane was a high-powered lawyer, with a husband and three kids, who was always overwhelmed with her to-do lists and suffering from burnout. The one task she always seemed to find time for was cleaning out her pantry. When I asked her why, she said that cleaning out the pantry was therapeutic. It was a purely physical task that was very gratifying because the results were so tangible (unlike a lot of the mental work she did as a lawyer and a mom). It was a thirty-minute escape that recharged her in a way that doing the crossword puzzle just didn't do. Once she saw this connection, she realized that exercise (something she never took time for) would give her a similar result—it was a purely physical activity that would refuel her for the constant mental stress that dominated her life. She began scheduling thirty-minute power walks at her lunch hour and found her energy levels at work and at home much improved.

WHAT'S NOT WORKING?

Now that you've seen that you actually are managing at least some of your time well and have some clues as to why, it's time to ask the next question: What's not working? The answers to this question may come more easily to you; after all, what's not working motivated you to read this book in the first place.

Still, it's helpful to write your responses down and take a look at the whole picture. It will be interesting to compare your answers to this question to your answers to the What's Working questionnaire.

Again, this can be a free-form exercise, or you can use the following sentence starters to help get you thinking.

EXERCISE # 2. WHAT'S NOT WORKING?

Fill in the blanks. Remember to consider all areas of your life. Try to think of as many examples as you can!

I never have time to _____.
I spend way too much time on _____.
I don't have well-defined goals for _____.
One thing I wish I could do every day is _____.
I always underestimate how long it takes to _____.
I procrastinate whenever I have to _____.
I am usually late for _____.
It's hard for me to say no to _____.
I have a hard time finishing _____.

Here are some sample answers:

I never have enough time to <u>exercise, relax, see my friends, prospect for new business, make follow-up calls.</u>
I spend way too much time on <u>cleaning the house, filing, processing e-mail, attending meetings.</u>
I don't have well-defined goals for <u>my personal life, my career, my finances.</u>

One thing I wish I could do every day is <u>play my guitar, exercise, nap, talk one-on-one with my kids, eat a sit-down lunch.</u>
I always underestimate how long it takes to <u>write a proposal, shop for groceries, review reports, plan a meeting, organize my closets.</u>
I procrastinate whenever I have to <u>start a new big project, pay bills, exercise, make collections calls.</u>
I am usually late for <u>work, appointments, the dentist, everything.</u>
It's hard for me to say no to <u>my boss, my kids, my spouse, persistent people.</u>
I have a hard time finishing <u>the laundry, thank-you letters, the dishes, big projects.</u>

Your answers to this question become your list of everything you want to fix. In this book, you will learn how to address all of these problems. Every so often, come back to this list and see how much progress you've made toward reaching your goals.

But before moving on, take a good look at this list and compare it to your list of "What's Working?" If you are having trouble starting or finishing certain tasks and not others, ask yourself why. In some cases, things aren't working because you need to develop certain skills, such as how to prevent interruptions or say no.

Can you identify a time in your life when you felt more in command than you currently feel? What changed? Are there old systems that used to work for you that you can go back to? It's not uncommon to abandon an old reliable system thinking there must be something better out there, but never find a replacement. For example, Paula always kept track of her commission sales in her old-fashioned paper planner. Seeing how she was doing over the month guided her decisions in how to spend her time. When she switched to a networked computer system, she stopped tracking her sales. She needed to go back to an old-fashioned planner for tracking sales so she could pace her activities appropriately over the month.

APPLY YOUR RESULTS

Once you know what's working and what's not, you can use the information to fix many of your time-management problems. Often we possess the time-management skills we need, but apply them only selectively. For example, if you are always on time for some things, but late for others, you have the capacity to be on time. You own that skill. You are simply choosing (consciously or unconsciously) when to apply it. Your job is to ask yourself what it is about the things you are always on time for that motivates you to be prompt. Then see if you can apply those principles to your problem areas.

GETTING REAL

Teresa, Children's Clothing Store Owner

Teresa owned a children's clothing store and worked long hours, leaving little time for errands and chores. She hated burdening her husband and kids with them and, truth be told, she worried that things wouldn't be done to her liking if she delegated chores. That said, the thought of tasks that often went undone was eating away at her, and she resented spending her few hours of free time on menial, though necessary, chores. Her "What's Working?" list revealed that she had no trouble delegating duties to her staff at work. I asked her why.

Teresa realized that she was able to delegate at work so effectively because she wrote out instructions and created simple forms for basic procedures. She recognized that she could do the same thing for many of her home-related tasks. By writing out instructions and creating simple checklists, she was able to delegate many of her household chores to her husband, children, and hired help.

YOUR TIME-MANAGEMENT PREFERENCES

Sometimes you struggle with some tasks more than others, not because you're lacking a skill, but because of individual preferences or the particular conditions under which those tasks occur. We all have unique preferences about when and how we do certain tasks or activities. When we honor those preferences, it's easier to get things done. For example, some of us like to work in short concentrated bursts; others need a longer window of time. Some people like to work in isolation; other people can only get things done by working with others. Some like last-minute pressure; others absolutely hate it. Tuning in to these natural inclinations can help explain why certain items keep landing on your "What's Working?" and "What's Not Working?" lists.

To help you discover the preferences and natural inclinations that affect whether or not you get to certain tasks and activities, do the following exercise. Preferences can change from day to day; as you answer these questions, think about how you feel *most* of the time.

EXERCISE #3. WHAT'S YOUR PREFERENCE?

Circle whichever answer rings truest for you. Don't edit yourself or prejudge your answers. There is no "right" or "wrong" (although some people might try to convince you that there are)—just go with your gut.

The majority of the time, I prefer . . .

Concentrating in short bursts	vs.	Concentrating for long stretches
Focusing on one thing at a time	vs.	Multitasking
A fast and busy schedule	vs.	A slow and easy schedule
Plans and predictability	vs.	Surprises and spontaneity
Tight deadlines	vs.	Long lead times
"Stewing" on things	vs.	Making quick decisions
Working independently	vs.	Working collaboratively
Exercising alone	vs.	Exercising with others
Relaxing alone	vs.	Relaxing with others
Working in silence	vs.	Working with background noise or music
Dim lighting	vs.	Bright lighting
Working with my head	vs.	Working with my hands

This information will help you plan a schedule that makes you happy and productive. If you thrive on a fast pace, you should try to fill your days with several activities; if you prefer a slower pace, you might limit your daily to-do list to three to four items. Stop trying to fight who you are. Someone who responds well to very tight deadlines should try to schedule his or her time that way. That is, create that pressure-cooker environment by telling yourself that you *must, must, must* finish whatever you're working on by 12 p.m. Schedule something critically important right after your self-imposed deadline to make sure you stick to it. It might feel awkward at first, but you will be creating the environment that produces your best stuff. Paying attention to your natural rhythms—and accepting them as a testament to who you are—will result in a schedule that supports you instead of one that works against you.

GETTING REAL

James, Computer Consultant

James was a computer consultant whose time-management skills appeared to be very inconsistent. When it came to client appointments, he was the picture of efficiency; he always arrived on time, was energetic and focused throughout the session, and got a tremendous amount done. Yet, when James was not with a client, in his own office, doing administrative or business-related duties, he puttered, procrastinated, and got very little done. No matter what was on his to-do list (bill paying, writing proposals, strategic planning), he'd waste half the day doing nothing. As a result, his business and self-esteem were suffering.

I asked James why he thought his time with clients was so much more productive, and he came up with two reasons: (1) James found contact with people very energizing; and (2) James was very responsive to the confined boundaries of the appointments. With a well-defined start and end time, he was able to focus and pace himself to make the most of the time allotted. How could he apply this insight to address what wasn't working?

During his days in the office, I suggested he create boundaries by assigning start and end times to each of the items on his to-do list—he'd write "Draft new brochure 10:00–11:00 a.m.," "Filing 12:00–12:30 p.m." directly into his planner. To give him the people contact he needed, I also recommended that he break up his solitary tasks with tasks that required personal contact. After forty-five minutes of concentrated work, he'd make a couple of phone calls to reenergize himself. Lunches with clients, prospects, vendors, or friends on "office days" would also provide an added reward and break. The combination of establishing

> structure around his to-dos and interspersing solitary work with people contact fueled James's energy and made his productivity on "office days" soar.

YOUR ENERGY CYCLES AND SOURCES

In addition to your natural preferences, your energy levels can have a profound impact on your effectiveness. Energy is power; it is the force that enables you to move toward your goals.

Once you recognize and understand your natural energy sources and cycles, you can begin to manage them. Without being tuned in, you may be trying to tackle your most challenging activities when you're feeling sluggish and wasting your peak energy on less demanding tasks.

Study yourself. Clues to your energy cycles and preferences often lie in the way your days operate. For example, if you keep promising yourself to wake up at 6 a.m. and work out, but haven't made it to the gym even once, it's probably a safe bet that getting up with the early birds just doesn't jive with your body. Or, if you volunteered for committee work at your kids' school, but always dread going to meetings, maybe you're more comfortable working alone than in a big group.

No matter how good your intentions are, if you're doing something at the wrong time of day when your energy level isn't quite right, you either won't do what you're supposed to or it'll take five times longer than it should.

Understanding your rhythms gives you a point of negotiation—you might not always be able to match with the optimal time to do them, but if you're aware, and willing to make a case for yourself, you can pull it off more often than not. Over the years, I have learned that I do my best creative thinking between 9 a.m. and 3 p.m. Therefore, I always schedule my writing, and even media interviews, for those hours. After three, my brain goes to mush and I must move on to different types of tasks. Periodically, I'll get an eleventh-hour request from a journalist on deadline requesting ten tips on organizing a closet or five ways to create a user-friendly filing-system. I know if I sit down at 4 p.m. to write it'll take me two hours, instead of the thirty minutes it would take me in the morning. I always ask if they can possibly wait until the next morning, when I have a clear head and can provide them with the highest-quality material. More often than not, the person can wait. You just have to know enough about yourself to make the request.

EXERCISE #4. IDENTIFYING YOUR ENERGY CYCLES

Complete the following sentences.

Mornings are the best time for me to _____.

And the worst time for me to _____.

Afternoons are the best time for me to _____.

And the worst time for me to _____.

Evenings are the best time for me to _____.

And the worst time for me to _____.

Late at night is the best time for me to _____.

And the worst time for me to _____.

YOUR UNIQUE ENERGY BOOSTERS

Since you can't always control when you do certain tasks, the best time managers are also very tuned in to what activities fuel their energy when it is flagging. This varies from person to person, so you need to think about what works for you. By knowing what energizes you, you can avoid energy drops throughout the day altogether and fully enjoy whatever you are doing, whether it's work or play.

Long days, a lot to do, pressure, eating on the run—all these can contribute to flagging energy. So can heat, humidity, monotony, boredom, dim lighting, staring at a computer screen for hours, jet lag, sleep deprivation, and certain medications. Some of these are an inescapable part of life, but avoid known energy drains when you can. When you can't, counter them with a potent energy booster.

EXERCISE #5. YOUR UNIQUE ENERGY BOOSTERS

When you're feeling sluggish, but have to perform, what works? Is it getting up and doing jumping jacks or a headstand, having an energy drink, calling a friend for a quick laugh? Circle those that work for you.

When my energy is flagging, I can usually recharge by:

- changing activities
- exercising
- stretching
- playing some music
- focusing on my goal
- glancing at a photo of someone I love

- drinking a glass of water
- taking a catnap
- eating a high-energy snack
- taking a brief break
- planning something fun
- calling a friend
- other

VARIETY IS THE SPICE OF LIFE

Sometimes, a change of pace is all you need to boost your energy. For example, if you have been doing quiet, concentrated work for hours on end and your brain desperately needs a break, it's a great time to do a task that requires you to move around and use your muscles. Similarly, if you have been doing mindless physical tasks all day (like stuffing envelopes for a mailing, or cleaning the house), your body may need a break, but your brain may be raring to go. Do a mentally stimulating task.

After a plethora of social interaction (like a full day of meetings, or a family gathering), give yourself time away from the buzz with a quiet task. Bottom line: When you plan your day, make sure you build in enough variety to keep yourself invigorated.

The key to *Time Management from the Inside Out* is to build your life as much as possible around your individual needs and desires. Once you've developed some basic time-management skills—and anyone can master them—you will have much more control over your daily, weekly, and monthly schedule. Then you will be able to factor in your energy levels, your preferences about pace and interruptions, and your energy ups and downs. Even when you cannot control your environment, it is helpful to know what's optimal for you, so that you can quickly identify what's working against you and compensate for it.

As you refashion your approach to time, you'll discover all kinds of interesting and wonderful things about yourself. Time management is the ultimate in self-improvement because it is the foundation that will enable you to achieve your goals in every aspect of your life.

But first, let's go one step further in understanding your unique situation.

In the next chapter, we're going to analyze how in or out of balance your current life is.

8

WHERE DOES YOUR TIME GO?

Because time is so intangible, it can be easy to misconstrue; you may think things are going one way, when in fact what's happening is quite different. Things we don't enjoy (like chores, or weekly staff meetings) feel like they eat up all of our time, but there's never enough for activities we cherish (like spending quality time with family, or doing creative work).

Can that really be true? Or are your perceptions off? The goal of this chapter is to give you an accurate picture of exactly where your time goes and how in or out of balance you really are.

SIMPLIFY YOUR CATEGORIES

In order to check your balance, we first need to establish exactly what you are trying to balance your time between. Everybody divides the departments of their life a little differently. One of the secrets of managing your time well is to simplify your life categories. Below are some common life categories. Choose the five or six from the list below, or come up with categories that make sense to you.

- Work
- Family
- Self
- Romance
- Friendship
- Finances
- Knowledge
- Home
- Spirituality
- Community
- Health

If you've come up with more than five or six categories, reexamine your list.

Just as a closet can only hold so many categories of belongings, you can only juggle your schedule between so many categories of activities. It would be cumbersome to organize your closet into ten or twelve sections: skinny belts, wide belts, dressy belts, casual shoes, work shoes, dressy shoes, short-sleeve print tops, long-sleeve print tops, short-sleeve solids, long-sleeve solids, heavy pants, medium-weight pants, Acck!! It's way too much to keep track of. It's far easier to maintain control over three to five broad sections: tops, pants, suits, dresses, accessories.

Similarly, it's much easier to manage your time and monitor your balance when you're juggling three to six broad life categories instead of fifteen small ones. If you've come up with too many categories, consider what might be bundled under a single umbrella. What can you combine? Perhaps health, spirituality, and friendship can be bundled under "Self." Maybe finances and knowledge can be subsumed under "Work." Do whatever seems most natural to you. Like this:

Author, Speaker, Single Mom (me)

- Work
- Child
- Self
- Relationships

Here are some other examples of life categories:

Sculptor, Single

Day job
Creative work
Family and friends
Self

Woman Exec, Married with Kids

Work
Marriage
Kids
Mother (aging, infirm mom)
Self

Divorced Dad

Work
Kids
Romance
Self

Retiree

Learning
Volunteering
Travel
Family/grandkids

What Are the Departments of Your Life?

This chapter's main focus is on your life outside of work, but you also need to balance your workdays between a variety of responsibilities. If you are having trouble managing your time at the office,

identify the core responsibilities you need to divide your time between. What does your employer pay you for? Why are you there?
What are your most valuable contributions? If you aren't dividing
your time properly between your various responsibilities, you
might feel out of balance.

Examples of work categories

Economist

Analytic work
Networking
Consulting/client work
Teaching

Social Worker

Patient care
Writing reports
Research on new support
 services
Continuing education
Family support

Salesperson

Customer appointments
Product research
Paperwork
Prospecting

Teacher

Lesson planning
Grading
Teaching
Counseling students
Extracurricular activities

What Are the Departments of Your Work Life?

_____

_____

_____

_____

_____

GO BACK TO THE CLOSET

If each week is simply a container into which only so much can fit, the next step is to take a closer look at where your time is spent. The idea here is to make plain exactly where your time goes—we've got to peek inside the closet of your week and see what's really going on. There are two ways to accomplish this check:

Option A: Study your planner for the past two weeks.
Option B: Track your time for one to two weeks.

If your stomach is already clutching at the idea of putting your schedule under this kind of intense scrutiny, I understand. The act of tracking your time can feel incredibly tedious and overwhelming, and may even stir up bad memories of a horrible micromanager from your past. Rest assured that no one has to look at your logs but you. The more willing you are to honestly look at where your time goes, the better position you will be in to make adjustments to create the life you want.

Another reason you may dread this exercise has to do with facing your own personal fears. What if you don't like what you find out? What if you discover that you actually *can't* do everything, or that you've been wasting a tremendous amount of time each week on things you just don't care about?

Facing the truth can be hard, but it is well worth the effort. By looking closely, you are likely to find hidden pockets of time you didn't realize you had, and certain activities and tasks that you can cut to make room for what's more important to you. And who knows, *you might be doing better than you think*. You'll never know until you look.

GETTING REAL

Lisa, Teacher—Hidden Pockets of Time

Lisa loved every element of her life—juggling children, job, home, and relationships. She told me there was nothing she was willing to give up. Yet she was always sprinting from one activity to the next, constantly running, and pushing everyone else in her life to run faster, too. Lisa's goal was not to do less but to manage it all with less stress. She longed to savor each moment of the wonderful life she had created.

I gave Lisa blank weekly schedules and asked her to track her time for two weeks. (Appendix A provides a blank Time Map.)

She found the exercise challenging. Beyond her work hours and her children's school and after-school schedules, Lisa was surprised to discover how little time she could account for. She realized that household chores and errands had no particular place in her schedule. Rather, she haphazardly squeezed them into any day, at any time, at any hour. She paid bills while sitting through her daughter's dance class, made phone calls from her son's baseball games, sorted her mail in the doctor's office.

No wonder Lisa couldn't enjoy the moment. She was never really in it!

Her first reaction was to feel overwhelmed. "How do we live like this?" she wondered. "When do we get anything done?"

Upon closer examination, we were able to make three significant discoveries.

1. Looking for something to cut, Lisa eyeballed three hours spent every Wednesday afternoon attending a training class for new teachers. When she'd first become a teacher, this

made sense, but she was about to begin mentoring new teachers herself. If she were to stop the class, she could create an oasis of time for herself in the middle of the week—to do anything she liked. Lisa loved that idea but was afraid she'd be tempted to fill the three hours with family errands. To guard against that, I suggested she create a limited menu of acceptable activities for that time slot; she chose antiquing, exercise, browsing in a bookstore, a manicure. Excitement reigned.

2. Fridays were comparatively calm, Lisa noticed, because everyone was home by 4:30 p.m. and there was no pressure to get homework done. A hidden pocket of time! We declared this as Family Night and then developed a routine that would become a welcome tradition: 4:30–6:00 Household Chores (with everyone chipping in); 6:30 Dinner; 7:30 Board Game or Movie Night. With all the chores and cleanup done, that family time could be sacred and undiluted by distractions and worries about anything she wasn't getting to.

3. Lisa still needed time alone with her husband. But Saturdays were extremely hectic, with Todd coaching baseball and games often going on until 7 p.m. We decided that going out every Saturday night would be too much, but alternate Saturdays would be perfect. For a weekly shot, Lisa decided to apply her parents' long-standing offer for babysitting to Mondays, a typically stressful day. If Lisa's parents took the kids out for dinner that night, she and her husband could enjoy being home alone together once a week. The kids and their grandparents loved the idea, and Lisa's schedule began to take a saner shape.

> The simple act of tracking her time for a week allowed us to initiate a few significant shifts in Lisa's life. Her days still felt full and rich, but with the added balance in her week, Lisa felt calmer. Lisa cherished those hours each week as her time to refresh and renew for the week ahead. She finally had time to live in the moment.

Are you ready for your close-up? Choose whichever tracking technique you're most comfortable with.

Option A: Highlight Your Planner for Two Weeks

If you are relatively diligent about using your planner for recording your to-dos and appointments, you can get a decent view of your balance by studying your planner.

Assign a different color highlighter to each of your life or work categories (e.g., work—blue; family—pink; self—yellow), then go through your planner and highlight each meeting, appointment, to-do, call, and activity with the appropriate color to indicate what's what. (NOTE: If something falls under two life categories, highlight it with both colors, in a striped pattern.)

This may not yield as accurate a read as if you tracked your time because your planner is likely to be missing some of the activities you really did do (e.g., interruptions and distractions, unplanned activities) and how long you actually spent on each task, but overall, it will give you a quick visual impression. To make the exercise more precise, think about time spent on anything (meal, activity, outing, etc.) that wasn't actually documented in your planner.

Now, look at this snapshot of your life. How balanced is it? Are there any surprises? Are you spending more time in one department than you realized, and less somewhere else? Is there an additional category of life you forgot to include in your original list?

Are there any hours you can't account for? What do you think is going on during that time? Is there any structure to your week at all, or is every day completely out of control? Are you wasting any free time, or are your days so tightly packed that it gives you a headache? Are there tasks that might be deleted or moved to give you more hours to work with?

Examine your daily to-do lists and see how many things you actually checked off. If you didn't get to your list or make it all the way through it, what stopped you? What derailed your schedule? Was it someone else's crisis? Aimless procrastination, like chitchat and surfing the Net? What else do you notice?

Option B: Doing the Math—168 Hours in a Week

There are 168 hours in a week. Find out the ratio of time you are spending on each department, by tracking your time for a week or two. Make a copy of the blank schedule grid below, or create a similar one on your computer. For one week (or two), keep close track of where your time goes every day. In the beginning you may feel like you're spending more time keeping track than anything else! But hang in there—the information you gain is well worth the effort.

As you track your time, be sure to tie each task and activity to one of your major life categories. You can be as general or specific as you like. If you tend to concentrate for long stretches on the same kinds of tasks, you can just block off whole hours and give them a category—work (9–5), sleep (11–6), family time (7–10 p.m.). If you tend to shift back and forth between life categories, making a personal call in the middle of your workday, or doing some work-related e-mail at night before you go to bed, tracking will require more work. Imbalances are often obscured by frequent shifts. If you can quantify the hours you spend on each category, you'll discover how truly in or out of balance you are. If you are scrutinizing the time you spend on the phone, try to indicate which department of your life a specific call belongs to. For example, if you make a call about your child's ice-skating lessons, mark it as "Family"; if you call to set an appointment for a massage, tag it as "Self."

Don't forget to account for time spent commuting and waiting. What do you do during that time? If you are reading for your job, tag it as "Work." Talking to your kids? Tag it as "Family."

Once you've tracked your time for at least one week (two is ideal), add up how many hours you spend on each department of your life. When you are done, divide each sum above by 168 (hours in the week) to determine the percentage of time you spend on each department of your life.

TOTAL: 168 hours

Work_____hrs._____%   Friendship_____hrs._____%

Family_____hrs._____%   Romance_____hrs._____%

Knowledge_____hrs._____%   Health_____hrs._____%

Finances_____hrs._____%   Other_____hrs._____%

Self_____hrs._____%

Common Stuck Points

Having a hard time accounting for the following?

Household chores: Consider which department of your life you attribute them to. If creating a peaceful, well-organized home is a source of joy and pleasure for you, either give it its own category, such as "Harmonious Home," or tag it as "Self" time (because it's something you do for your own peace of mind). If caring for your home is one of the ways in which you create a warm, inviting family life, tag it under "Family."

Activities that fall under more than one life category: You may find that some activities fall under more than one life category—taking a brisk power walk with your daughter may be "Health" (fitness) and "Family." I say, the more activities that fall into more than one category, the better! When it comes time to calculate, either split the time between the two categories, or count it under whichever department you consider the dominant goal.

At the end of the week, evaluate your log:

1. How do you spend most of your hours?
2. What departments of your life are completely neglected?
3. Is your schedule balanced?
4. Are there any surprises (i.e., you thought you spent more time with your kids than you actually do)?
5. Is there a structure to your week or is it somewhat random?
6. Are there any hours that you cannot account for?
7. Any patterns?
8. Are you happy with how you spend your time?
9. How do you decide what has to be done on a daily basis?
10. What throws your schedule off? How do you deal with interruptions and unexpected requests?

Then search for:

- **Hidden Pockets of Time.** Look for hidden pockets of time (that aren't being utilized). What could you use them for?
- **Things to Cut.** What activities might be deleted or moved to help restore the balance? Are you doing chores out of habit that you might be able to delegate or eliminate altogether? Are you spending time on activities that you've outgrown?

- **Time of Day.** If any task or activity took you much longer than anticipated, were you trying to do it at an unrealistic time, given your body's energy cycles or other demands of that time of day?
- **Pace.** Do you feel like you never have time to stop and think? Is there enough relaxation time, or alone time, built into your days? Clearly you won't be able to do it all, but have you carved out enough time in each day, or week, for what's most important?
- **Routine.** Did you really get up and go to sleep when you planned to? Did you struggle to keep your categories separate and distinct from one another? Were you constantly switching gears, hopping from one department of your life to the next in a matter of seconds? Taking personal calls in the middle of your workday, or dealing with work issues after-hours, are just two of several ways to blur those lines.

BALANCE AS AN INDICATOR OF GOAL CLARITY

Checking your balance will also provide an interesting view of not just your time management challenges, but also the clarity of your goals. It's been my observation that the areas we spend the most time on are the areas where our goals are the most clear. If your life feels out of balance, look to see where you are spending the majority of your time. Chances are that your time is being spent in those areas of your life for which you have well-articulated goals. For example, if work takes the majority of your time, your work aspirations are probably crystal clear, whereas your goals for your personal life (which you rarely make time for) are less developed.

I've always believed that if you aren't where you want to be, you're either on your way or you're not so sure you want to get there. If you say you want to exercise, but aren't making the time, ask yourself if you are ambivalent about being in top shape. If you keep promising yourself to make time for your friends but never do, you must ask yourself if there is something about those relationships that makes you anxious.

Pay attention to the areas that monopolize your time. Are those where your goals are the clearest? In order to truly create balance in your life, you need to clearly set goals for each department of your life. Part 4, "Strategize: Designing the Life of Your Dreams," will help you define those goals and make them clear and specific so you can create the life you desire.

PART IV
STRATEGIZE

Designing the Life of Your Dreams

9

DEFINING YOUR GOALS
AND ACTIVITIES

What's it all about, Alfie?
—Burt Bacharach/Hal David

Your dreams and desires are the heart of time management from the inside out. I wholeheartedly believe that you can accomplish just about anything you want when you set your mind to it. First, you must be clear on what you want.

It's time to step away from the daily details and take a bigger-picture view of your life. When you look at the big picture of life and think about what you want, you get in touch with your deepest values, the fundamental things that will make you happy.

There are two steps to strategizing and defining the life you want:

1. Defining your big-picture goals
2. Selecting activities to help you achieve those goals

This chapter will help you focus and define what you really want out of life. Chapter 10 will help you design a schedule to make it happen.

DEFINING GOALS AND ACTIVITIES

Let's begin by defining the difference between goals and activities.

- A goal is the destination. It's *what* you want to achieve.
- An activity is *how* you get there. It's the specific means to your higher goals.

Big-picture goals are based on your core values, and they tend not to change much over the course of your life. For example, warm and loving relationships, well-adjusted kids, financial security and wealth, expertise in a particular area, an inviting and comfortable home, a sense of connection to your community—they are all values you are likely to hold on to throughout your life.

Activities (how you choose to achieve those goals) do change over the course of your life. There are many ways to achieve any one big-picture goal. For example, you can gain a sense of community by volunteering, attending religious services, organizing the block party every year, becoming the neighborhood's hangout house. You can maximize your health by working out, meditation, eating healthily, and getting regular checkups.

People often confuse activities with goals. If you've ever heard yourself make such New Year's resolutions as "My goal is to exercise three times a week," "I am determined to spend more time with my family," "This year I'm going to look for a new job," and found yourself unable to stick with your commitment, it's because you were focusing on the activity, not the goal. Exercise, spending time with family, and job hunting are activities, not goals.

The question is *why* do you want to do these things? What is the purpose of exercise? Motivation to take action comes when you see something on the *other* side of the activity that you really desperately want. Why exercise? To feel stronger. Why spend time with family? Because you want to feel a sense of connection. Why search for another job? In order to provide for a more secure future.

So, be sure to distinguish between a big-picture goal—the point of it all—and an activity, which is what you use to get there.

To give your life focus, we are going to first define your big-picture goals and then, in the next chapter, choose activities that will help you achieve those goals.

DEFINING YOUR GOALS—LET YOURSELF DREAM

To feel nourished, energized, and balanced, you need to set big-picture goals for each category of your life. Many of my clients set career or financial goals, but neglect to set goals for other critical areas of their lives. If your life feels out of balance, look to see where you are spending the majority of your time. Chances are that your time is being spent in those areas of your life for which your goals are clear-cut.

In chapter 8, you identified the five or six major departments of your life. (If you didn't read chapter 8, answer the question now: How do you divide your life? What are you trying to balance your life between?) You probably are juggling at least some of the following:

- Work
- Finances
- Family
- Knowledge
- Self
- Home
- Romance
- Spirituality
- Friendship

Now look at your major life categories. Consider your deepest values and ask yourself, "What would make me happy in each of these key areas of my life? When all is said and done, what am I working toward? What do I dream of attaining in each life department?"

For family, Diane wrote: "I want a home that is a warm, inviting place for my family to live and to spend time with friends." Terrence's big-picture family goal was: "To make my kids feel really loved and important." For work, Alan, a caterer, chose: "I want to be recognized as the most innovative caterer in the city." Jill, a lawyer and mother, combined career and family goals into one: "I want work that nourishes me, while leaving me time to nourish my children." Pauline's big-picture relationship goal was: "To make sure my husband always knows how happy I am I married him." Maria's big-picture knowledge goal was: "To become an aficionado of theater."

Write down just one or two big-picture goals for each major life category. Don't belabor the language, and don't make a big list. You don't have to do it all. You just have to do what's really important. Get quiet with yourself, and ask, "What's it all about, Alfie?" Keep your big-picture goals simple and heartfelt. You don't have to think about *how* to get what you want. All you need to say is *what* you want in the broadest terms.

WRITE IT DOWN, MAKE IT HAPPEN

Writing down your big-picture goals is essential to making them come true.

In a well-known study of the Yale class of 1953, the recent graduates were questioned about their future plans. Only 3 percent had written out their goals and plans of action. Twenty years later, this 3 percent appeared happier and more content than the others; furthermore, this small group had achieved more wealth than the remaining 97 percent of their classmates put together.

When you put your goals in writing, opportunities to realize your dreams begin to present themselves to you, almost as if by magic. Some people say that's because when you put your goals in black and white, you begin to attract what you need. I have a different theory. I believe we are surrounded by opportunities to achieve almost anything we want every day of our lives. But we don't notice them; it's all a big blur. Once we have written down our goals, and made them clear, we begin to notice the specific opportunities in our path that will help us get where we want to go. Clarity of goals produces clarity of vision.

Jack Canfield and Mark Victor Hansen, authors of *Chicken Soup for the Soul*, set a tremendously ambitious goal of selling 1.5 million copies of their first book in a year and a half. Each of them wrote the goal on an index card and reviewed it a minimum of four times a day. Did they achieve their goal? In eighteen months, they sold 1.3 million. Pretty darn close. Danielle Steele had a twenty-five-year goal of selling 500 million books; she made it.

Copy the following chart. Write each of your life categories in one of the circles. Write your big-picture goals in the frames. Our next job is to find the activities that will help you achieve those goals.

Alternatively, take out a piece of paper and make a list of your life categories and alongside them your big-picture goals. Our next job is to find the activities that will help you achieve those goals. If you are having trouble defining your goals, be sure to spend some time reading the next few pages.

Maximize Health

Loving Relationship

SELF

ROMANCE

? ?

?

FAMILY

FRIENDSHIP

Well-adjusted,
Self-confident Kids

Close Connections

WORK

Reputation for
Excellence

HAVING TROUBLE DEFINING YOUR BIG-PICTURE GOALS?

There are many people who find articulating their goals difficult. There are whole books written on the subject of defining your dreams. Authors who have written excellent books on this topic include Barbara Sher, Brian Tracy, Cheryl Richardson, and Martha Beck.

I believe that all of us at our core know what would make us feel joy and contentment, but many of us are afraid to give ourselves permission to achieve what we really want. Remember that the truth—what you really want and believe—is always there, whether you acknowledge it or not. What is in your heart will direct your decisions, with or without your cooperation. If your dream is to start your own business, but you won't acknowledge that, and you insist on working for someone else, you will always feel conflicted and unhappy. Your body is going right, and your heart is pulling you to the left; or your body is going left and your heart is tugging you to the right. You have a choice to make: Either pay attention to what your gut is telling you and be one with the truth, or disregard it and find yourself in eternal conflict.

Sometimes clients are afraid to articulate their goals because they are afraid of locking themselves in or picking the wrong ones. They may feel so overwhelmed with choices that they think they can't possibly narrow them down. They're consumed with self-doubt. "Well, I think that's what's most important to me, but I don't know if that's right," or "My mother/husband/wife thinks I should do this," or "Do I really have the right to want that?" or "Is it wrong to want this much alone time?" Even worse, they question whether they're smart enough, or deserving of such happiness. They may feel so worried that they aren't capable or worthy of what they want, they don't dare wish for it.

Release the constant, frantic search for someone else's approval and acceptance of what you desire. This is your life, these are your dreams, and you deserve happiness. Don't worry about locking yourself into anything. Instead, pick one or two goals to achieve *for now,* knowing that you can change your mind about this if you discover along the way that it's not really what you want. Remember that life is nothing more than a series of decisions and corrections. There is no right answer.

You also need to give yourself permission to release goals that you really don't want. If you've had a goal on your list year after year, but have never made any steps in that direction, it may be time to reexamine whether that is something you really want. For example, when my daughter was younger, "Romance" was one of my departments and I set goals for it (gotta get out there and date, go out and meet people). In practice, though, I did nothing about it. I'd date the men who jumped out in front of me to attract my attention, but I never invested any time looking for a relationship.

Applying my own maxim—if you're not where you want to be, you're either on your way or you're not so sure you really want to go there—I finally asked myself why I wasn't making any moves. The answer was—I wasn't ready. The energy and attention I wanted to invest in my business and in my role as a single mother did not leave enough time to pursue a serious, committed, long-lasting relationship. So I took it off the list. My plan was to start the project up again when Jessi was in her last year of high school. That way, I figured, I'd be all set by the time she left for college. Pretty cocky, right?

Taking it off my list was liberating. I could stop beating up on myself for not pursuing a particular goal every year, and just concentrate on the life I was choosing to lead. I think you have to give yourself permission to not go someplace, to take it off the list. I don't think it should be a negative process (i.e., Geez, I'm giving up on myself). On the contrary, it's honoring that inner voice that says, "I am not ready for that." Stop pressuring yourself to go there, and instead invest time asking yourself why.

Still stuck? Try one of the following exercises to get to the core of what you want.

Forgotten What Makes You Happy?

Exercise #1: Keep a Joy Journal

If you've been so focused on taking care of other people that you've lost touch with what makes you happy, try keeping a "joy journal" for a month or so. Start paying attention to what delights you. Observe yourself closely, and throughout the day. Whenever you notice you have just done something you've enjoyed, jot it down in your journal. Those activities are usually indicators of what makes you happy at your core and can bring you closer to the discovery of your goals. Give yourself permission to love what you love, whether it is cleaning out your refrigerator, reading poetry, or painting your kitchen.

Periodically review your joy journal and see what you learned about yourself. For example, one entry may be "Helped Susan figure out a management problem with her staff. Loved helping a friend, feeling useful, and coming up with creative ideas." What goals might come from this? Perhaps you will decide that you enjoy problem solving or counseling. Maybe these activities should be a part of your work, and maybe you need to make more time in your life to be with your friends.

Consumed by Self-Doubt?

Exercise #2: Crystal Ball

Maybe you feel you are so far away from where you would like to be that you can't allow yourself to acknowledge your dreams. If it's hard for you to define openly what you want out of life right now, try thinking ahead to the distant future.

Picture your life ten years from now. Look into a crystal ball, and fantasize what your life would look like if you could have anything you want. Give yourself permission to want what you want. Don't judge your dreams as they enter your conscious mind or they'll never make it onto your list. Don't worry about what is possible yet; just dream, and dream big. Your fantasies should be loose and free—the grander, the better, as long as they sound wonderful to you.

Once you can see it, write it down. Divide a piece of paper into two columns. On the left, list each of your major life categories. On the right, write what you see yourself doing in the crystal ball. You might write:

Major Life Category	Ten Years from Now
Self	"I am traveling extensively."
Family	"I am married to someone I love, and I will have three children."
Work	"I am running my own business."
Finances	"I have a huge investment portfolio."
Community	"I live in a small town where I am surrounded by friendly, caring people."

Now, look at the items in the right-hand column. Those are your goals. That's what you want. The next step is to figure out how to get you there. That's a matter of selecting the right activities.

CHOOSING YOUR ACTIVITIES

Once you know what your big-picture goals are, you need to choose a few specific activities that will help you to achieve these goals. Unlike big-picture goals, which tend to stay the same year in and year out, the activities you choose to accomplish these goals will change as needed. They may change annually or more often as you move closer to your goals, accomplish what you set out to do, or discover a better path to your goals.

Since there are endless ways to achieve any one goal, you may need to brainstorm first and then narrow down your choices from there. For example, if your goal is to challenge yourself intellectually, you could do that through a variety of ways going back to school, reading a book a month, or attending six lectures and seminars per year. If your goal is to build wealth, you might choose to develop a budget and cut expenses, or learn about the stock market so that you can begin investing in it, or find an investment adviser.

For each big-picture goal, generate a list of activities that will help you get there. Be as specific as possible. Here are some examples.

Major Life Category	Big-Picture Goal	Specific Activities
Self	Maximize health	• Get more sleep
		• Exercise three times a week
		• Plan a vacation around a favorite activity (such as skiing or hiking)
Family	Well-adjusted kids	• Daily one-on-one time
		• Help with homework
		• Weekly family outings
Work	Fulfilling career	• Improve skills
		• Job hunt
		• Network
Marriage	Exciting marriage	• Daily talks with spouse
		• Weekly dates

		• Private weekends away
Home	Warm, welcoming home	• Daily pickup of clutter
		• Weekly cleaning
		• Redecorate
Friendships	Close, connected network	• Weekly talks or e-mails
		• Buy ticket series for local music or sports events with a friend
		• Monthly get-togethers
Finances	Build wealth	• Invest 20 percent of each paycheck
		• Read *The Wall Street Journal*
		• Research new business idea
		• Pay bills on time
Community	Make a difference	• Volunteer to coach a children's sports team
		• Donate clothing and food

You will probably generate so many activities that you can't begin to pursue them all. If your list includes eight things to do to develop a fulfilling career, ten steps to build wealth, and fifteen ways to make your children feel loved, you'll have to pare it down. Focus on the top two or three choices in each category and postpone the rest. Any more than three or four activities per category will be too overwhelming and throw your schedule out of balance. Just do the math: If you have six departments of life and three activities per goal, that's eighteen activities, each of which you'll need to find a place for in your schedule.

If you are unsure of how to pursue one or two of your goals, talk to friends for ideas, or make researching the goal one of your activities. For example, you may want to start a home-based business, but you don't know what it will take to make that happen. In that case, your specific activity may be to read some books on the topic, do some Internet research, or network with other small-business owners to find out how they got started.

Now, take the two or three activities you have chosen, and write them on the lines between your goals and life categories (see page 170). This completed image is the snapshot of what you want to accomplish and how you will get there.

REVISE YOUR LIST OF ACTIVITIES ANNUALLY

Your big-picture goals will rarely change because the things you value will tend to remain constant throughout your life (for example, you may always want solid friendships, well-adjusted children, and financial security). However, the way you strive toward your big-picture goals will change regularly. You will replace some of the specific activities you've chosen from year to year as you achieve some of your smaller goals and outgrow other activities. You may instinctively reevaluate your activities at particular times of the year—in January, as the new year begins; in September, when you're in a back-to-school mode; or, if you live in a cold climate, in the spring, when the warm weather and sunshine return and energize you to start planning new projects.

Changes in your life circumstances also can affect which goals dominate different times in your life. When your kids are young, their well-being may take precedence over your career fulfillment.

Once you have built wealth, you may choose to spend more time on activities related to self-fulfillment.

At least once a year, reevaluate your activities. For each big-picture goal, ask yourself, "How will I pursue this goal this year?" If one of your goals is to have a warm, welcoming home, here is how your specific activities might evolve from year to year.

Big-picture goal	*Warm, welcoming home*
Year	**Activity**
Year 1	• Organize main living space and closets
	• Develop routines for maintaining clutter-free home
	• Keep house clean; hire housekeeper to clean once a week
Year 2	• Tackle attic, garage, and basement
	• Adapt family cleaning routines to accommodate new family schedule (youngest child goes to kindergarten, husband working fewer hours, etc.)
	• Begin hosting club meetings at our house twice a month
	• Redecorate first floor
Year 3	• Remodel kitchen
	• Host dinner parties twice a month
	• Build deck
Year 4	• Landscape front and sides of house
	• Plant vegetable garden in back of house

For some people, the process of defining goals can be eye opening, forcing them to focus for the first time on what they really want in life. For most people, though, it's less a surprise than it is a process of clarification. You probably already had a pretty good idea of what your goals were, even if you'd never written them down, so it's likely that the actions you have chosen were also familiar to you. In fact, you are probably already engaged in some of these activities. On the other hand, many of my clients are surprised at how many things they aren't getting to. They've corrected imbalances like that with Time Maps that designate slots for things that they've established as top priorities. The next chapter will show you how you can do it, too.

10

TIME MAPPING: CREATING YOUR IDEAL BALANCE

Achieving balance means dividing your time into the right proportions for you. In the previous chapter, you identified big-picture goals for each department of your life and selected activities that would help you achieve those goals. The next step is to design your schedule to make time for those activities.

This chapter is dedicated to Time Mapping, a technique that helps you create the balance you need to bring renewed energy and satisfaction to every part of your life.

WHAT IS A TIME MAP?

A Time Map is a budget of your day, week, or month that balances your time between the various departments of your life. Built around your own custom set of priorities and choices, your Time Map reflects who you are and what is important to you.

Obviously, any one of the roles you play might be a full-time occupation—being a good parent, spouse, relative, employee, boss, or friend could easily consume all of your time. A Time Map prevents one department of your life from monopolizing all of your time.

A Time Map provides structure to your day and week, which frees you to live in the moment, because you know in advance that everything has a time and place in your schedule. Think back to school, when your day was organized into clearly distinct class periods: art, science, social studies, English, math, lunch. These subdivisions allowed you to focus on each class one at a time. If in the middle of history class, you came up with an idea for your art project, you wouldn't just get up, walk down to the art studio, and begin sculpting. You'd keep taking notes on the rise and fall of the Roman Empire, knowing that there would be a time for you to work on your creation in fourth-period art. A Time Map works similarly. By carving out distinct times for each of the departments of your life, you can relax and fully enjoy each moment, because you know every core activity has its time and place in your schedule.

A Time Map is also a powerful tool for becoming a proactive agent amid the whirlwind of demands that come your way. Instead of feeling that you have to act on every request the minute it crosses your path, your Time Map guides you, helping you determine whether you have time to handle an unexpected task, how much time you will devote to it, and when you will do it. When you don't have a Time Map, you have no idea what to do when. Every day is a total free-for-all. You just say yes to whatever screams loudest, with no perspective on how to prioritize incoming requests or when you should be doing things.

With a Time Map, you know where each request fits into your overall plan. When life throws you curveballs, you know what they're diverting you from. This enables you to make a conscious choice about whether you're willing to be diverted, and if so, what you'll get back to later. You also feel motivated to postpone some things to a future hour, day, or week, because you will want to preserve the carefully constructed balance you have achieved.

Summary: Benefits of a Time Map

- Ensures balance
- Guarantees time for your core activities
- Allows you to live in the moment
- Provides a framework for daily decision making

Time Maps: Constricting or Liberating?

The idea of Time Mapping almost always produces a mixed reaction from audiences I present to. Why? While many people are receptive to structure imposed from the outside (e.g., most of us respond well to regular work hours), we're not as comfortable imposing structure on ourselves. You may find yourself bucking at the idea of constricting your life so much.

A Time Map involves taking control of your schedule—exercising your power to say yes, and no, and be in charge. Some, especially those who thrive on routine, love this idea and can't wait to design their own Time Maps; others sit writhing in their seats, sure such a structure will destroy their creativity, or be impossible for them to implement.

Rest assured that a Time Map can be adapted to any personal style, whether you thrive on routine or variety, whether you have complete or only partial control over your daily schedule. The key is simply this: You're the only one who can create a structure for your days that best suits you.

Later in this chapter, I'll identify less traditional Time Mapping techniques, designed especially for people who like to maintain maximum flexibility.

TIME MAPS REFLECT YOUR PRIORITIES AND GOALS

Here are the Time Maps of three people who live very different lives. Notice how the amount of time spent on each life category varies from person to person. What can you learn about each person's priorities from looking at their schedules?

Erin, Entrepreneur and Marathoner (p. 177)

If you noticed right off the bat that Erin is only sleeping five hours per night, please recognize that I'm not advocating everyone try to operate on this little sleep. Erin was a marathon runner, and this happened to be all the sleep she needed. Getting up this early to fit in a long run was what fueled her for the day. The rest of her Time Map allotted ample time for all the passions in her life—work, kids, and husband. This was the balance that worked for her.

William, CFO of a Major Manufacturing Company (p. 178)

When William and I started working together, he had been struggling to juggle his time between career, family, kids, and a secret dream project—to write his autobiography. He'd been trying to squeeze writing in whenever he had a spare moment—after work, a periodic quiet Saturday morning, or Sunday afternoon. Unfortunately, this haphazard approach produced almost no book pages in two years. We created a Time Map that carved out routine writing time six days per week, barely intruding on the other departments of his life. One hour every morning from 7 to 8 a.m. (after the kids already left for school), and five hours on Saturdays from 7 a.m. to 12 p.m., which still left him lots of family time. With this new Time Map, William had three chapters drafted within the first three months.

⏱ **Time Budget** ⏱

Erin—entrepreneur, marathoner
Married, no kids

Time	Monday	Tuesday	Wednesday	Thursday	Friday	Saturday	Sunday
5:00 a.m.	Wake Up	Wake Up	Wake Up	Wake Up	Wake Up	Wake Up	Wake Up
5:00–8:00 a.m.	SELF—running	WORK—strategic planning	SELF—running	WORK—strategic planning	SELF—running	SELF—running	SELF—running
8:00–9:00 a.m.	SELF—shower/dress						
9:00 a.m.–12:00 p.m.	WORK—admin	WORK—client appointments →		→	→		
12–12:30 p.m.	Lunch						
12:30–	WORK—marketing	WORK—client appointments →	→	→	WORK—Marketing	FAMILY—chores/errands	ROMANCE/FRIENDSHIP outings with friends
6:00 p.m.	Dinner						
6:00–7:00 p.m.							
7:00 p.m.–	ROMANCE—relaxation	WORK—networking	ROMANCE—relaxation	WORK—networking	ROMANCE/FRIENDSHIP—dinner with friends	ROMANCE—evening together	FAMILY—paperwork—bills
10:00 p.m.	Sleep	Sleep	Sleep	Sleep	Sleep	Sleep	Sleep

ERIN'S TIME MAP

William—CFO, manufacturing
Married, 3 kids

Time	Monday	Tuesday	Wednesday	Thursday	Friday	Saturday	Sunday
6:30 a.m.	Wake Up	Wake Up	Wake Up	Wake Up	Wake Up	Wake Up	Wake Up
6:30 - 7:00 a.m.	SELF—Shower, dress, breakfast					SELF— Writing autobiography	FAMILY— spirituality, church
7:00 - 7:30 -							
7:30 - 8:00 a.m.	SELF—Writing autobiography						
8:00 - 8:30 a.m.	COMMUTE—reading						
8:30 - 9:00 a.m.	WORK—e-mails						
9:00 a.m. - 12:00 p.m	WORK—internal meetings; calls				WORK—Sign Checks		
12:00 - 1:30 p.m.	SELF—lunch/gym					FAMILY— games, shopping, kids events	FAMILY— fun day
1:30 - 5:30 p.m.	WORK—external meeting, offsite appts						
5:30 - 6:30/7:00 p.m.	WORK—e-mails, calls; daily tie-up				ROMANCE— dinner w/wife		
6:30/7:00 - 7:00 p.m.	COMMUTE/KNOWLEDGE—Business reading					ROMANCE— date night	FAMILY/KNOWLEDGE— quiet time, reading at home (board mtg 1x/mo)
7:00 - 7:30 -							
7:30 - 9:00 p.m.	Family—dinner, homework w/kids				FAMILY— evening w/kids		
9:00 - 9:30 -							
9:30 - 11:00 p.m.	ROMANCE—marriage time						
11:00 p.m.	Sleep	Sleep	Sleep	Sleep	Sleep	Sleep	Sleep

WILLIAM'S TIME MAP

Samantha, Neonatal Nurse

Samantha's husband, Tom, was in the Coast Guard and traveled for four to twelve weeks at a time, four times a year. Working the second shift gave Samantha the flexibility to see her kids off to school, tuck them in at night, and have enough time during the day to take care of the household (preparing dinner, running errands, and paying bills). Her mother watched the kids for four hours every afternoon, between the time they got home from school (about 6:30 p.m., post–after-school activities, sports practices, etc.) and the time Samantha got home from work around 10:30 p.m. She would take two hours, after packing the kids off to bed, to relax and prep for the day ahead. It wasn't ideal (she would have loved to be with them after school), but that wasn't the reality of her family's situation; at least this way, she could maintain a careful balance between her life and her kids'.

GETTING REAL

What Can Derail You?

A Time Map is your default template. It's the framework into which you place all the tasks that you do. It is your anchor and your compass in the storm of activity demands, and opportunities swirling around you. Will you be able to use it 100 percent of the time? Of course not. On average, your Time Map should work about 80 percent of the time. Twenty percent of the time, you'll have to toss your plans to the wind and deal with the urgency of the moment.

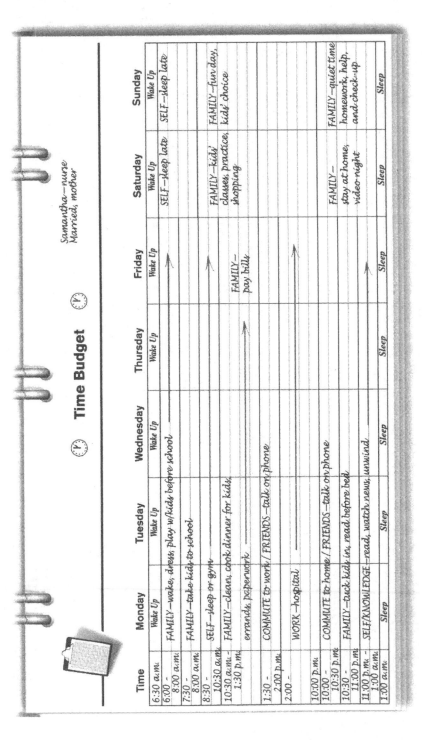

SAMANTHA'S TIME MAP

BEFORE AND AFTER TIME MAPS

Time Mapping brings us back our closet metaphor: It's all about arranging everything you want to do within the confines of your week. If your personal balance checkup in chapter 8 revealed anything from a slight imbalance to a big chaotic mess, a Time Map can be used to correct it. The examples below illustrate three instances in which the use of a Time Map solved a specific problem, either at home or at the office.

Jason, Attorney, Pro-bono Counsel for a Nonprofit

When Jason hired me, he, like so many of my clients, was in big trouble at the office. He was a brilliant attorney (he'd breezed through law school in two years!), but he hadn't been billing enough hours for his firm and felt like he wasn't getting anything done. I asked him to identify the departments of his work. He easily ticked off: Clients, Speaking/Marketing (he delivered several speeches each month on behalf of the firm), and Staff. A big part of his day was also dedicated to pro bono work for a nonprofit; it was a huge responsibility that included correspondence, preparing contracts, and doing media interviews. Page 182 is what the "closet of his week" looked like before we started working together:

Jason's clear passion was for the pro bono work. Every morning he'd log into his work e-mail and spend fifteen minutes dealing with firm matters. Then, he'd open his nonprofit e-mail, to just "check," but end up spending a couple of hours going back and forth on strategy with the executive director instead of doing work for the firm. After 9 a.m., it was a free-for-all—he'd do anything that came at him, in no particular order. We needed to establish some structure to his workday that would guarantee more billable hours, time for lunches with the firm partners (so he could repair relationships), and leave enough time for his pro bono work.

Jason's Time Map BEFORE:

☉ Time Map ☉

Jason—attorney

Time	Monday	Tuesday	Wednesday	Thursday	Friday	Saturday	Sunday
6:00 a.m.	Wake Up	Wake Up	Wake Up	Wake Up	Wake Up	Wake Up	Wake Up
6:00 – 6:15 a.m.	SELF—wake up, Blood sugar, Brush teeth, Pack lunch						
6:15 – 6:45 a.m.	COMMUTE—SELF—phone calls to friends, Pro-bono						
6:45 – 7:00 a.m.	WORK—E-mail						
6:45 – 7:00 a.m.	PRO BONO—E-MAIL						
9:00 a.m. – 7/9:00 p.m.	Anything that comes at him / PRO BONO—CLIENT MATTERS—SPEAKING—MARKETING						
7:00 – 7:30 p.m.	COMMUTE						
7:30 – 11:30 p.m.	HOME						
11:30 p.m.	Sleep	Sleep	Sleep	Sleep	Sleep	Sleep	Sleep

Jason's Time Map AFTER:

⊙ **Time Map** ⊙

JASON—attorney

Time	Monday	Tuesday	Wednesday	Thursday	Friday	Saturday	Sunday
6:00 a.m.	Wake Up	Wake Up	Wake Up	Wake Up	Wake Up	Wake Up	Wake Up
6:00–6:30 a.m.	SELF—Shower, Dress, Pack lunch						
6:30–7:00 a.m.	COMMUTE						
7:00–							
11:00 a.m.	Client matters						
11:00 a.m.– 12:00 p.m.	Client calls/e-mails (East Coast)						
12:00– 1:00 p.m.	LUNCH—firm relations					Errands	
1:00– 3:00 p.m.	Speaking						
3:00– 5:00 p.m.	Pro bono					Class	
5:00– 7:00 p.m.	Client calls/e-mails (West Coast)						
7:00– 7:15 p.m.	WRAP-UP, Plan next day						Fun/Friends
7:15–7:45 p.m.	COMMUTE						
7:45–8:30 p.m.	DINNER						
8:30– 11:30 p.m.	SELF—relaxation					Friends	Prep for week
11:00 p.m.	Sleep	Sleep	Sleep	Sleep	Sleep	Sleep	Sleep

With this schedule in place, Jason's productivity increased dramatically. We got him working on client matters first thing, so that by 11 a.m. he'd already billed a solid 4.5 hours. He postponed doing any work on behalf of the nonprofit until 3 p.m. (this was when his energy started lagging anyway, and those two pro bono hours were a good pick-me-up). Within three weeks of implementing this plan, he billed more hours than he had in the previous two months combined. His clients were pleased with the speed and quality of his work, the lunchtime hours (set aside to reconnect with the partners) seemed to be improving his standing, and the nonprofit was getting even more of his concentrated time than before.

Allie, Working Mother of Four

Allie, the mother of four school-age kids, had a Time Map in place that worked well for her until she reduced her work schedule from full-time to three days a week. She suddenly had Mondays and Fridays off—two whole days—but was surprised to discover that with all that extra free time, she was barely getting anything done!

Allie thought the two extra days at home would give her more time to relax, tend to ongoing household projects, and actually get enough done during the day to really focus on being with her kids in the evening and on weekends. But now that she finally had the time to oversee a landscaping renovation and catch up on her reading, her days still got away from her. Somehow this new-found "freedom" was hijacked by mundane tasks like laundry and cleaning. The informal approach to her days at home wasn't working.

Allie and I created a new Time Map for her Mondays and Fridays (the two problem days), with the goal of getting the most out of that time.

Time	Monday	Tuesday	Wednesday	Thursday	Friday
7 a.m. to 9 a.m.	Drive kids to school, laundry, and housework				Drive kids to school, laundry, and housework
9 a.m. to 12 noon	Personal projects				Personal projects
12 noon to 3 p.m.	Errands time				Self time

Allie's Monday and Friday Time Map

After dropping her kids off at school, we built in one hour of meal prep, laundry, and house cleaning. Nine a.m. to noon each day was saved for home projects, into which Allie could plug any of her personal projects. Then, every Monday from 12 to 3 p.m., she'd run household errands (instead of running out whenever she thought of something). From 12 to 3 p.m. every Friday, Allie took time for herself—she'd have lunch with a friend, read a book, or go for a walk—it was her time. The structure we put in place ensured she would maximize her productivity with these two days off, and the "Self" time on Friday was a reward at the end of the week that gave her something to look forward to.

Miranda, Financial Planner

Miranda's main responsibilities as a financial planner were to (1) recruit new clients, (2) meet with existing clients, (3) do market research, and (4) design and manage client investment portfolios. She was so committed to accommodating her clients that whenever a client or prospect called to request an appointment, she'd say, "Okay, when would you like to meet?" Miranda always agreed to whatever time and day they asked for, even if she had planned to work on something else (like strategizing a portfolio design and doing market research, which were time-consuming, concentrated tasks). Eventually, the anxiety about the neglected portfolios built up and Miranda would end up staying at the office until midnight a couple of nights a week trying to catch up.

I suggested that she set aside a specific time for client meetings and a specific time for project work each day. Since her clients almost always requested morning or early-evening meetings, Miranda honored that preference by reserving every morning and two evenings a week for client meetings. To maintain a balance, she reserved three hours each afternoon for project work, such as designing her clients' portfolios and market research.

Now, when a client requested a meeting, Miranda had a more proactive way of responding. Instead of asking an open-ended "When would you like to meet?" she'd ask, "Are mornings or early evenings better for you?" When all her morning and evening appointments were booked, she'd say, "Let's meet next week." If Miranda really wanted to accommodate a special client who needed an afternoon appointment, she could give up one of her financial planning sessions, but it would be a conscious decision. Then she'd work on portfolios one evening or morning to make up for it.

Use a Time Map as much or as little as you want to. As the anecdotes above illustrate, some people like having a Time Map for their workdays, while others only need one to help plan out a few days a week. Look to the place in your life (work, home, or both) where some activity or to-do is being left out. Use a Time Map in those areas, to fit in everything you desire.

	Monday	Tuesday	Wednesday	Thursday	Friday
Time 9 a.m.	Client visits	Client visits	Calls	Client visits	Design time
	↓	↓	↓	↓	↓
	↓	↓	Paperwork	↓	↓
	↓	↓	↓	↓	↓
	↓	↓	Client visits	↓	Calls
	↓	Design time	↓	Design time	↓
	↓	↓	↓	↓	Client visits
	Calls	Calls	↓	Calls	↓
6 p.m.	↓	↓	↓	↓	↓

INSTANT BALANCE FIX

In chapter 1, I asked you to name one thing you were not getting to. Maybe you wanted to spend more time with your spouse, or with your children, or with your friends. Maybe it was time for a personal passion or hobby. Maybe it was time to manage your finances. Experiment with the idea of Time Mapping by adding in just that one activity.

Locate a regular time in your day or your week that you can throw a net around, and claim as your sacred time to tend to that one activity. No matter how haphazard the rest of your week is, carve out this one oasis of order—a regular appointment with yourself to exercise, relax, or get critical work done. See what it feels like to build a little routine into your schedule. Notice how satisfying it feels to know that you are carving aside the time you need for the most essential, missing ingredient in your life.

Years ago, I was a single mom with a young child and a new business. My schedule was packed full—and quite organized—with time set aside for all the aspects of running my company and giving my daughter the time she needed. What was missing was any time for myself. I needed to find something that wouldn't take much time, but would give me a little restorative oasis in my week. One thing that had always brought me joy was dancing. I started to go swing dancing one evening a week, Sunday nights. I basically shoved a little Self Time into an already packed schedule.

Believe it or not, adding that one thing totally transformed my life. My energy, speed, and productivity the rest of the week were catapulted onto another plane. Making room for this fun escape, this balancing element, created more time in the rest of the week. I suddenly had more time on my hands than I ever had in my life. Looking forward to Sunday nights gave me energy when dealing with my business and my daughter. Savoring the memories of the previous Sunday kept me going for days afterward. I felt satisfied, whole, balanced, and refreshed. It was amazing!

That's why it's so important to build balance into your life. Whatever you've been neglecting needs a safe and protected place in your schedule. It will free you from the guilt of not getting to it. It gives you something to look forward to. It gives you a feeling of control over your life. It will introduce you to the concept of being proactive and taking charge.

Whether it's time for yourself, or time to pay bills, start your Time Map by finding and claiming a time in your schedule every day or every week to do it. By adding this one ingredient back into your life, you may suddenly and magically restore your sense of equilibrium and everything else will fall into place. This regular appointment with yourself can show you the freedom and benefits that come from imposing a structure to your week from the inside out. This kind of structure doesn't enslave you, but propels you toward your life goals and liberates you to feel good about how you spend every day.

CREATE YOUR TIME MAP

Now it's time to build a schedule that reflects your priorities and carves out time for everything that you deem important and essential.

In chapter 9, you defined your big-picture goals and identified the specific activities that support those goals. You will need this information to proceed because now you are going to block out regular times in your schedule for each of those activities.

Start with a blank schedule (copy the blank Time Map in appendix A), take out a pencil, and begin mapping. Fill in the time you wake up, the time you go to sleep, and all of the constants in your life: work hours, classes, regular doctor appointments, mealtimes (if you always eat at the same time every day).

The time in between is what you have to work with. Start transferring the activities from your lists into your schedule. This is where you decide how much space each activity will take up in your day, week, or month.

Let's take the "Maximize Health" goal from the example in chapter 9 to illustrate how scheduling activities works.

Major Life Category	Big-Picture Goal	Activities
Self	Maximize health	Get 8 hours sleep
		Exercise 3×/week
		Eat home-cooked meals

On your new Time Map block out your eight hours of sleep, designate three specific times to exercise each week, and schedule cooking time daily to prepare the healthful meals you want to eat.

If you've never had any structure to your week, you may not be sure when the best time will be for you to do certain tasks like chores or hobbies. In deciding when to schedule each activity, be realistic. Think back to chapter 7, when you learned about your personal energy rhythms. That will guide you in determining whether to get your eight hours by going to bed earlier or getting up later, whether to work out at the beginning of the day or the end, and how to schedule time to prepare those home-cooked meals.

Also take into consideration other realities in building your schedule. For example, if one of your activities is to play your cello at least four hours a week, you could schedule a large two-hour time block twice a week, or you could play for one hour at a time on four separate days.

Designing your Time Map is like working out a puzzle—you might need to move things around a few times in order to get it right. Continue this process for all of your big-picture goals until you have scheduled time for each activity.

LAYERING ACTIVITIES

As you fill out your Time Map, there is a good chance you will run out of space to put things. If you have more activities than time, one option is to layer activities. You can make bill-paying time more restorative by playing some fabulous classical music, spraying some aromatherapy mist into the air, and enjoying a frothy chai tea. You schedule phone calls to friends and family while washing the dishes (a headset or ear piece makes that possible). You can catch up on your reading by listening to books on CD while commuting.

Don't feel like you should always layer your activities. Sometimes it's nice to keep your time simple and focused. You are in charge of your time. Squeezing in multiple activities at once may help you get a lot done, but it could also lead to your feeling frenetic and exhausted. Find a balance between multitasking and simple focused time that's right for you.

Once you've set up your Time Map, follow it for a couple of weeks. See how it feels. After you have seen it in action, you will be in a better position to evaluate it and make adjustments.

HATE STRUCTURE?

This section is for those readers who can't even begin to fathom using a Time Map. Some people have a fear of structure—they are certain that routinizing their days would squelch their creativity and spontaneity. Others believe the concept is wholly unrealistic. "There's *no way* I can exert that much control over my schedule!" they say. "My life just doesn't work like that." I hear you. But both of these fears, while real, don't preclude you from using some system to assert some control over your overall balance.

Before I got organized, one of the biggest obstacles I had to overcome was a belief that I wouldn't be the same, creative person if I sacrificed my chaotic ways. I thought I was at my best when pulling things off at the last minute, getting projects in barely under the deadline. It seemed to me that my creativity derived from the fact that I was constantly flying by the seat of my pants. I was dead wrong. The truth is that by managing my time better, that is, by creating certain routines in my workday and family life, I actually had more creative energy to devote to higher goals.

The three alternatives to the Time Map presented below will help you stay in balance, without forcing you to abandon your flexible, spontaneous self.

Alternative #1: Balance Tracker

This system works especially well for people who know what they need to balance their time between, but don't like being bound by any one thing at any particular time. I developed this concept for an advertising executive who prided himself on a free-flowing, laidback style. Julian was committed to maintaining that relaxed vibe, but he wanted to ensure he was balancing his time among the departments of his workday. He tucked his Balance Tracker into his jacket pocket each week and simply marked a box whenever he spent any portion of an hour on one of the major departments. Each box represented one hour. If he spent a half hour, he'd strike a diagonal line through a box; if fifteen minutes, a short line. His goal, more or less, was to have every box checked off by the end of the week. So, if it was Thursday, and he noticed that he'd been neglecting an entire department, he could adjust his schedule to guarantee that he got to it before the end of the week. The card helped Julian track his time, but still granted him the freedom and flexibility that he thrived on. You can apply the same concept to your whole life.

JULIAN

AT WORK	WHOLE LIFE

AT WORK

WORK WEEK—50 hrs.

Strategic Planning—12 hrs.
□□□□□□□□□□□□

Managing Staff—18 hrs.
□□□□□□□□□
□□□□□□□□□

Admin—3 hrs.
□□□

Board of Director Duties—10 hrs.
□□□□□□□□□□

Idea Generation—7 hrs.
□□□□□□□

WHOLE LIFE

WEEKLY BALANCE—168 hrs.

Work—50 hrs.
□□□□□□□□□□□□□
□□□□□□□□□□□□□
□□□□□□□□□□□□□
□□□□□□□□□□□□□

Sleep—56 hrs.
□□□□□□□□□□□□□□
□□□□□□□□□□□□□□
□□□□□□□□□□□□□□
□□□□□□□□□□□□□□

Exercise—3 hrs.
□□□

Meals—12 hrs.
□□□□□□□□□□□□

Spouse—20 hrs.
□□□□□□□□□□
□□□□□□□□□□

Kids—27 hrs.
□□□□□□□□□□□□□□
□□□□□□□□□□□□□

Alternative #2: "Sudden Opportunity" List

If you are a crisis manager—someone whose job or life revolves around managing volatile or unpredictable factors—your schedule can't be neatly designed around predetermined time zones. Maybe you're a mother with very young children, or a doctor, or a reporter, and you find yourself perpetually "on call." Whatever your role, the point is that you never know when you might have a free minute. So when you do happen to find yourself with an empty fifteen-minute slot, you could end up wasting it wondering what to do.

The idea behind a Sudden Opportunity list is to be prepared to make the most of every free moment of time. Your list can either be organized by how long an activity takes (see below) or may simply consist of one thing (e.g., doctors use every free moment to fill out patient paperwork; a traveling salesperson picks up messages and returns phone calls between every appointment).

Creating this list will take the indecision out of your free moments, so you can actually get something done. Anytime you think of something you need to do, ask how long it will take and assign it to a list (remember to break up big projects into small chunks of time). Then, when you get an unexpected break, go to your five-minute, thirty-minute, or one-hour list and pick a task.

- **Five minutes or less.** Make a quick phone call, read an article, back up some files on your computer, write someone a birthday card.
- **Thirty minutes or less.** Read a report, update your expense reports, cook dinner, clear out a file drawer, go for a walk.
- **One hour or less.** Search the Internet, work out, do a load of laundry, work on your business plan, pay your bills, get a haircut.

Alternative #3: Time Map for Alternative Work/Life Rhythms

Just as some people's lives lend themselves wonderfully to short blocks of structured time, others are just the opposite. If your work, or life, demands long stretches of uninterrupted time, you might consider creating a Time Map where each "day" is dedicated to a different activity. When your time is laid out in twenty-four-hour cycles instead of short spurts, it allows those who thrive on immersing themselves in whatever they're doing to do just that.

Brendan was a professional sculptor. He designed pieces to sell at local galleries, but he was spending a significant amount of time on a park project commissioned by the city. Because his work was so labor- and energy-intensive (he specialized in steel works), there was no way he could physically dedicate several hours each day to his art.

I helped him design something called a vertical Time Map. Instead of assigning time for the same activity each day (e.g., working out from 7 to 8 p.m. on Monday, Tuesday, and Thursday), we assigned each day its own activity. He spent Monday and Tuesday working on independent gallery projects. Wednesday was a day off to rest, run errands, and see friends. All day Thursday and Friday morning, he worked on the park project, leaving Friday afternoon, Saturday, and Sunday to catch up on things around the house and restore his creative juices for the following week.

A TIME MAP REFLECTS WHO YOU ARE

The amount of structure you create within your Time Map will depend on your personal preferences. Even after you've set it up, you have flexibility in how closely you will follow your Time Map. If you thrive on structure, follow it to the letter. If you prefer more flexibility, you can be looser with it.

Let's say you have designated Sunday evening for home improvement projects. As ideas come to you throughout the week, such as painting the bathroom, organizing the garage, and catching up on photo albums, there is no need to agonize over when you are going to squeeze these things in. Open your planner and find an available Sunday, and schedule it in.

If you decide you can't wait till Sunday to work on those photo albums, feel free to do it sooner, switching it out with something else on your Time Map. For example, you may decide to do it one evening when your kids are sleeping over at friend's house—and devote that Sunday evening to family time instead. That's the beauty of a Time Map done properly: It's a truly customizable tool that you use in the way that works best for you. The key is to have a baseline from which to make decisions, thus providing you with the flexibility you need.

Adjust Your Time Map Until You Can Answer "True" to All These Questions

T F My Time Map reflects my big-picture goals.

T F My Time Map includes time for all the categories I want to get to.

T F I am able to concentrate on my chosen activity (during family time, I can concentrate on my family; during work time, I can focus on my work).

T F I am doing my activities at the right times for me.

T F My schedule makes me feel balanced and energized.

If it doesn't meet all the criteria, keep tweaking it until all the pieces fit to your satisfaction. Remember that time management is a fluid process. Your job is to protect and monitor this "ideal" at all times. Accept the fact that your Time Map will not work all the time but that it's something you should always come back to.

Now that we've completed this big-picture view of your life, it's time to go back down to the details. Part 5 of this book, "Attack: The SPACE Formula" will teach you how to honor your balance while managing the daily onslaught of distractions, demands, and ideas, all of which will threaten to throw you off track. The SPACE Formula will protect your balance no matter what kind of Time Mapping system you've decided to use.

PART V
ATTACK
The SPACE Formula

11

SORT

By now, you've developed a big-picture view of your life by defining your goals and activities and selecting a balance-tracking tool such as a Time Map, Activity Card, or Sudden Opportunity list. The question is how to make these tools work for you in the real world.

It's time to come back down into the details and apply what you've learned to connect your daily tasks to big-picture goals.

Let's be clear on how daily tasks are distinct from, but intimately connected to, your big-picture goals and activities. As you may recall from chapter 9,

- A *big-picture goal* is a destination, *what* you want to achieve. (For example, fitness)
- An *activity* is *how* you get there. (For example, exercise)
- A *task* is a specific component of an activity. (For example, running on the treadmill, resistance training, hiking)

Put another way, your activities are of a general nature (studying for your MBA, writing letters, spending time with your kids, cleaning your home). Your daily tasks and to-dos are the specific elements of each of those activities (phone calls, meetings, chores, errands, letters, and conversations). On a daily basis, you need to decide *which* letters to write; *which* chapter to study; whether to read to your kids, play a game, or go to the park; *which* room in the house to clean and how significantly. But for a meaningful and fulfilling life, each daily task can and must be tied back to your chosen activities and big-picture goals.

The SPACE Formula—Sort, Purge, Assign, Containerize, Equalize—will help you accomplish this. In my first book, *Organizing from the Inside Out,* I introduced the SPACE Formula for digging through the physical clutter. If you were organizing a closet, here are the steps you'd take.

Sort—Group similar items.

Purge—Eliminate the excess, the duplicates, as well as the broken, meaningless, and archaic items.

Assign—Give a specific home for each item you have decided to keep.

Containerize—Keep your categories separate with dividers, bins, and baskets.

Equalize—Refine, maintain, and adapt your system to reflect your changing needs

Since organizing time is like organizing space, it follows that the SPACE Formula can be applied to your tasks as well. Here's how to apply the SPACE Formula to organize the tangle of to-dos that come your way:

- **Sort**—Group potential tasks by life category and goal.
- **Purge**—Eliminate the excess, the duplicate, meaningless, ineffective, cumbersome tasks.
- **Assign** a home (a specific day/time) to the tasks you decide to do.
- **Containerize** tasks to keep them within the time allotted.

- **Equalize**—Refine, maintain, and adapt your schedule to your changing needs.

Part 5 teaches you how to apply the SPACE Formula to your daily tasks, starting with this chapter, "Sort." Keep in mind that although part 5 devotes an entire chapter to explain each step of the formula, what I am really teaching is a very rapid thought process. Once mastered, Sort, Purge, and Assign happen in an instant. Containerize lasts as long as each individual task you are doing, and Equalize becomes an ongoing part of your life. The SPACE Formula for tasks happens daily and constantly.

In order for the SPACE Formula to work, it's essential to have the following tools visible and handy:

- Your planner
- Your list of big-picture goals
- Your Time Map, Balance Tracker, Sudden Opportunity list (or whatever tool you've chosen to use to track your balance)

These tools will be your main "filtering device" for all the decisions you have to make when it comes to how you spend your time on a daily basis.

Every day, you face myriad choices about your daily to-dos. There are things you have to do, things you want to do, and things other people ask you to do. There are opportunities and distractions that arise each time you read a book or magazine, surf the Net, or attend a meeting, party, or conference. There are the internal interruptions that halt the progress of the task at hand (sudden inspiration, the desire to procrastinate, the need to stretch or get a drink), and external interruptions (other people's demands, unexpected e-mails, telephone calls, drop-ins, etc.), not to mention the unanticipated complications. Sometimes those can generate a whole other set of tasks and to-dos.

When looking at a long list of to-dos, it can be tempting to dive right in, starting at the top. But don't. Take a moment to sort through them to ensure you make wise and meaningful choices.

You have exerted great effort thus far to identify your big-picture goals, and to pick specific activities to achieve those aspirations. That was the tough part! Now your job is to stay true to yourself by implementing all of that good, thoughtful work.

The focus during the Sort phase is to simply categorize each task to determine if and where a task fits into your life.

For every task and to-do that crosses your path, ask yourself three questions:

1. Which of my big-picture goals will this help me achieve?
2. Where in my schedule does this task belong?
3. How long will it take?

You aren't deciding whether to do it yet or not. You job is simply to determine whether it warrants further consideration. Keep in mind that this is a simple thought process; it only takes a minute.

QUESTION #1
WHICH OF MY BIG-PICTURE GOALS WILL THIS TASK HELP ME ACHIEVE?

Seeing the connection between every item on your to-do list and your big-picture goals is essential to managing your time from the inside out. It will make you feel good about where your time goes, excited to wake up and start each day.

For every call, letter, chore, task, and interruption that crosses your path, ask yourself which life category it falls under and whether it will help you achieve what you want in your life. What is the relationship between this to-do and such goals as inner peace, wealth, and community connections?

For example, a financial publication arrives in your mail. Reading it is something you are considering. But don't just read it without thinking. Ask yourself which big-picture goal it might contribute to. If "Personal Finance" is one of your categories, you may think that reading about it (and learning a thing or two) will help you toward your goal of building wealth. Or, a neighbor asks you to help coordinate a fund-raiser for the neighborhood park. If one of your life categories is "Community," you may feel that getting involved would help you achieve your big-picture goal to make a contribution.

The point is to question each and every task so that you are conscious of why you would even consider doing it. You should never put anything on your schedule that you cannot connect to one of your big-picture goals.

Do you ever feel like your days are so filled with things you have to do, that you don't have time to get to the things you want to do? If so, you are failing to connect your daily to-dos to your big-picture goals. The truth is, we don't do anything we don't want to. Sometimes in the moment, we forget why we want to do certain things, especially the things we don't really enjoy. You can convert the have-tos into want-tos. In fact, in order to feel good about your days, you must do that.

Let me give you an example. Not long ago, my assistant and I were on our way back to the office following a meeting uptown. With several critical tasks to complete that afternoon, I was looking forward to getting back to the office as soon as possible. My assistant suggested we take the subway in order to avoid the heavy traffic. The drawback was that the train would leave us five blocks away from the office. Her argument was that since the weather was beautiful, we could enjoy the walk. With so much to do that afternoon, enjoying the weather wasn't at the top of my list. In fact, it didn't exactly fit in with any of my big-picture goals. However, being fit is one of my goals, and I could turn the have-to (we have to take the subway because the traffic is so bad) into a want-to—a ten-minute power walk in the middle of my day will contribute to my fitness goal. That small shift in my thinking put me into a proactive, positive frame of mind. Instead of feeling stuck or victimized by the traffic, I felt energized and excited about the walk. Connecting your choices to your goals gives you energy and power. You're in control.

When I teach this concept, there are usually a few cynics in the audience who raise their hands in protest. "No, there are things I do just because I have to." Like what? "Like laundry!" comes the response. "I don't want to do the laundry. I have to do it!"

Doing Laundry: Have-to or Want-to?

The truth is, you don't actually have to do your laundry. As a professional organizer, I can assure you that I've had clients who so abhorred this task, they simply never did it. They wore the same clothes over and over for a month or more until they couldn't take it anymore. Some clients actually went out and bought more clothes when they ran out of clean ones. (Come on, 'fess up. You've done that at least once in your life.)

Sound disgusting to you? Sound like an enormous waste of money? You want to feel clean and proud as you travel through the world, you say. Then the fact is that you are choosing to do your laundry. Which big-picture goal does doing the laundry help you achieve? Financial security (by not wasting money on last-minute replacement clothes)? Polished image? Social connections (who'd want to get close to you if you looked all disheveled and smelly)?

You can also apply this principle to unexpected situations that initially put you in a "have-to" frame of mind. Let's look at an example:

Staying Home with Your Sick Kid!
Have-to or Want-to?

Let's say you wake up one weekday morning, chomping at the bit to get to work (because you are very behind), but your child says he's feeling sick. No temperature, but his stomach hurts and he's looking rather green and pitiful. Oh, no. Now you have to stay home with your kid. You feel frustrated, victimized, and a tiny bit resentful. But why? The truth is, you don't actually have to stay home with your child. You have other choices. You could send him to school hoping he'll feel better, knowing that the nurse will take care of him if need be. You can hire that babysitter down the street who is always available but you've never liked very much. Or, you might even bring your child to work with you and let him sleep on your office floor.

But you choose to stay home. Why? Because you want your child to be comfortable, and staying home with him connects directly to your big-picture goal of making your child feel loved and important. And in the grand scheme of things, in this moment, this is your choice. Life doesn't always present easy choices. But once you make up your mind, take ownership of it. Connect to your choice. You'll suddenly realize how much control you really have. Attitude is everything.

You should never put anything on your to-do list that you don't want to do. No matter how miserable the task, take a moment to connect it to the why. Which big-picture goal will it help you achieve?

Connecting Your Daily To-dos
to Your Big-Picture Goals

Exercise: Take out your planner or to-do list for today. Write how each item connects to your big-picture goals.

Task	Which Big-Picture Goal?
_____	_____
_____	_____
_____	_____
_____	_____

QUESTION #2
WHERE DOES THIS TASK
BELONG IN MY SCHEDULE?

You've taken the time to create a schedule that provides your ideal balance. Whether you've opted for a traditional Time Map or a more creative balance-tracking tool, do a quick mental check to determine where this task would ideally fit into your schedule.

By doing this mental check, you'll get a sense of how this task is going to affect other things you have planned.

Let's look at a sample to-do list:

To-Dos	Where in Schedule?
Buy milk	Saturday—Errand Time
Get together with Jeannie	Friday night—Friendship Time
Register for business conference	Thursday afternoon—Planning Time
Clean out pantry	Sunday evening—Project Time
Make dentist appointment	Any lunch hour—Self Time
Update résumé	Thursday morning—Writing Time

Now, just because you have identified where the task fits into your schedule doesn't guarantee you'll be able to do what you want to do, when you want to do it. When you're dealing with other people (whether they are your coworkers, boss, family, or friends), there's always the possibility that someone will request you do something when it's best for them, regardless of how convenient or inconvenient that time is for you. For example, your son may need a new baseball glove for tomorrow's game, but your family "Errand" time isn't for another two days. Or the organizing meeting for the park fund-raiser is on Sunday night, but your community time is on Tuesday and Thursday evenings. If the task doesn't fit into your schedule as planned, does it mean you don't do it? Not necessarily. You may still choose to take your son shopping today. Asking yourself where the task fits into your schedule is just the opening line of an internal dialogue that will help you determine whether you'll do it, and, if so, when.

Asking where a particular task fits into your schedule also puts certain options in immediate perspective and helps you discover quickly if you are overloading a particular department of your life. Let's say one of your big-picture goals is to build financial security. Your neighbor invites you to attend a seminar about day-trading. You'd love to learn about the topic, and it seems to fit in with your big-picture goal of achieving financial security. But when you consider where in your schedule this would fit, you realize there is no space for it. You've already set aside seven hours per week for the Financial department of your life: six hours per week moonlighting to get out of debt and one hour every Saturday to pay bills, monitor your budget, and read up on basic money management.

This all-day Saturday course would throw your balance out of whack, replacing essential family time. At least for now, there's no room in your schedule to learn about and monitor stocks, so you decline the opportunity. Remember that you carefully chose activities that will help you meet your big-picture goals. You will undermine your efforts if you take on extra tasks that aren't part of your overall plan. If the task doesn't have a home in your schedule, that's an indication that it doesn't align with your chosen activities.

Finally, by figuring out where in your schedule a task belongs, you are in a position to compare it to other similar tasks so that you have a new perspective on whether it is worth doing compared to your other options. It's like organizing your closet and trying to decide whether you really need to hold on to a particular pair of jeans. Considered on their own, it's hard to determine whether to keep them or not. But by grouping them together with all the other jeans in your closet, you have perspective. You can suddenly see how this pair of jeans compares to the others. This pair may not fit as well; that one may look a little outdated; a third pair may be just right. Grouping tasks positions you to make wise, informed choices.

Next you need to consider how long it will take.

QUESTION #3
HOW LONG WILL IT TAKE?

Chapter 3 taught you how to estimate tasks, but here is your opportunity to truly leverage this new skill. The length of time a task takes in relation to its contribution to your big-picture goals is a primary factor in deciding whether it's worth doing.

There are many ways to achieve each one of your goals. If a potential task has passed the first two tests, estimating the time will position you to judge its value in relation to other options. Let's say you're trying to decide between a fifteen-minute task and a three-hour one. Both are directly related to the same big-picture goal, both will help you achieve what you want, but one takes twelve times longer than the other. Which is the most efficient and effective way to achieve this goal? Is there an even faster and more efficient way to achieve the same goal? Which do you choose?

Here's an example of some tasks that made it onto a small business owner's to-do list, all pegged for his Marketing Time. His goal: To increase business. How can he achieve that?

Assemble postcard mailing	5 hrs.
Write newsletter	10 hrs.
Call top 10 percent of customers and offer referral discount	2 hrs.

Examining these options in relation to one another will help this business owner decide where to invest his time. Looking at this list, the obvious choice may be the telephone campaign, requiring the least time (and dollars) and the biggest payoff: qualified new customers. However, he may decide that he wants to appeal to a new type of customer, and so a postcard mailing to a purchased list is the most efficient way to achieve his goal. (Writing the newsletter could do the same but would require much more time.)

Here's an example of similar tasks that all qualify for a two-hour block of Self Time you've carved out on Saturday afternoon. Your goal: Fitness.

Self Time

Swimming	2 hrs. (includes shower and hair-drying time)
Power walk with a friend	1 hr.
Yoga tape	½ hr.

In looking at this list, you might consider what you are in the mood for and which will give you the biggest return on your investment of time. You may decide, for example, to opt for the power walk with a friend, which will meet two goals (fitness and friendship) and give you time for lunch with your friend as well. Or, you may prefer the swimming option, which takes longer but will provide you with a healthy dose of the meditative, solitary time you crave.

The Sort phase is the first step in maintaining the balance you have worked so hard to design for yourself. Asking Questions #1–3 in this chapter will help you pare down your options. Even so, you'll have way more to-dos than time to do them in. Now, on to Purge, where we'll discuss how to overcome the psychological hurdles of letting some tasks go.

12

PURGE

As you know from chapter 4, when you have more tasks than time, you have four options:

1. Delete tasks.
2. Diminish tasks.
3. Delegate tasks.
4. Delay.

Acting on any one of these options can be fraught with confusion and guilt. It's hard to let things go from your schedule because, to some degree, we'd like to believe we *can* do it all. It's time to zero in on the psychological aspects of the four Ds. We need to move you past the guilt, fear, and uncertainty of each one so you can stay focused on the tasks and activities that are most critical to achieving your big-picture goals.

DELETE TASKS

Often, you will need to delete perfectly appealing tasks from your list simply to keep your life balance. Every working parent knows this. He or she is juggling several full-time jobs—raising kids, building a career, managing a household—any one of which could monopolize all the available time. If you have many roles and responsibilities, you will inevitably have far more potential tasks in each category of your life than you could possibly carry out.

When deciding what to toss, ask yourself which tasks carry the most impact, which choices will help you accomplish your goal most effectively and efficiently. Will any of the tasks you are considering help you accomplish more than one goal? The more goals a given task will help you accomplish, the greater its value to you.

Let's say you've set aside three hours every Monday afternoon to make sales calls. You've generated a list of thirty prospects but know you can call only about twenty in a three-hour period. You decide to let go of the ten cold calls and just phone the hot prospects.

Or perhaps you have designated Sundays for family outings. Your family comes up with three different ideas for the upcoming Sunday: seeing a movie, having a picnic, or going for a bike ride in the local nature reserve. Since another one of your goals is to get in shape, biking wins out.

The Art of Saying No

More often than not, the act of eliminating tasks involves saying no to other people. If it's hard for you to say no, you will end up doing things you don't really want to, simply because you feel guilty declining. We all hate to disappoint, but the larger truth is that those requests arc going to keep coming your way. Do you really want to spend your ever more precious time doing things just to please others? You need to learn how to balance doing things for those you care about, while still honoring your own goals.

To do this, you must recognize your right to say no. Only you have your eye on your big picture. Only you can decide what fits into your Time Map and what doesn't. Saying no doesn't mean you need to be abrupt or rude; you can get the message across in a perfectly polite and considerate way. You're also not obligated to go on at length about why you are saying no. You might want to explain, particularly if you are talking to a friend or someone else with whom you have a close relationship, but don't feel you have to.

There's a saying: "Stress is when your gut says no, and your mouth says yes." Touché! You usually know when you'd *like* to say no, but if it's not natural for you to refuse people, you find the words "yes, of course I will" popping out of your mouth. Practice smiling and calmly saying "I'm sorry, I just can't" and "No" out loud, looking at yourself in the mirror. Say them with a confidence and clarity until they feel natural.

Think about the people and situations you are most likely to say yes to instinctively. Compose a few tailor-made answers in advance and memorize them, so you won't be caught off guard. Here are some ideas to get you started.

Practice Saying No

- To decline an invitation for a party or event: "Thank you for thinking of me. I'd love to attend, but I have a prior commitment."
- To the head of the PTA. "That sounds like a great project, and I'm flattered you think I am the best person to handle it, but I'm too busy to do it justice right now. My schedule is already jammed."
- To a solicitor asking you to make a contribution: "I plan my charitable donations at the beginning of the year, and I never vary from it. Please remove my name from your list."
- To someone who keeps insisting: Just smile and keep repeating, "I'm sorry, I can't," "No thank you," and the good old standard:

"No." Don't explain further or you might be outmaneuvered, as the other person finds yet more reasons why you should be able to accommodate the request.

In some situations, it really is hard to say no. How do you say no to your boss or a client who (perhaps unwittingly) is saddling you with an impossible load? Ask the person for help in prioritizing the tasks. Present the situation in a calm, nonjudgmental manner, and suggest how the problem might be resolved: "I know you want me to do X, which will take five hours, and I'd be happy to do Y, which will take me about six hours. The challenge is, I can't do both before the end of the day. Which is more important to you? Or can we find someone else to take on at least a piece of one of these projects? Or can we wait a day on one of these projects?" Then honor the person's decision. The key is making other people aware of how long it will take to do what they are requesting. They won't know it, but you'll be teaching them the number one gateway skill to good time management

GETTING REAL

George, Teacher, Volunteer Extraordinaire

George was driven to effect positive change in the world and prided himself on his ability to support people through difficult times. Helping people reach their goals and making a contribution is what gave his life meaning and value. A career educator, he worked in tough inner-city public schools. He loved being on the front lines, inspiring achievement in literacy in as many kids as he could reach.

In addition, George volunteered as much of his after-school time as possible. He became a mentor for younger teachers, accepted a nomination to be on the City's Reading Council, chaired a committee to organize a statewide Read-In, and consulted for other inner-city school districts. On top of that he had responsibilities at home, which included coaching his daughter's soccer team and being a deacon at church. But he still felt like he was never doing enough.

George's schedule was so overloaded that he didn't have time to concentrate or really connect to any one thing he was doing. He staggered from one task to the next, never taking any time to reflect, and spent his nights worrying about what he wasn't doing or couldn't get to. He asked me to "help him become more efficient" so that he could keep doing it all, but with less stress.

George was trapped in an old-school belief that value and validation come from being able to do for others. His father had been a reverend, and his two older siblings had also chosen careers in service, but this deep-seated need to do for others was taking a physical toll on George.

After a few hours of my most persuasive arguments, I finally convinced George that value doesn't come from doing a zillion things at once and pleasing everyone. It's derived from a personal, concentrated connection to what one does best. He wasn't serving anyone if he worked himself into a heart attack or such a state of depression that he'd have to quit it all.

I asked him what he wished he could say no to. Though his response was barely audible, it was immediate: (1) his role as church deacon and (2) his committee chair position for the statewide Read-In. He'd served as deacon for many years, attending meetings every Thursday night (which kept him out until 11 p.m.) and getting to church every Sunday morning by 8 a.m. It was a political position that required navigating delicate relationships and mediating between several difficult personalities. The emotional energy required of his day job left him too depleted to handle this demanding interpersonal task.

The committee chair position was just beginning. George had been critical in securing the funding and approval of the event, and then they begged him to take over as chair. At the time, he felt he couldn't say no. But he dreaded the time commitment before him: eight weekends over the next four months, daily correspondence with administration officials, coordination of committee members, and months of follow-up after the event.

With my encouragement, George gathered the courage to say no and resign these two positions. First at the deacon's meeting, then at the monthly Read-In meeting, George explained that he was stretched too thin; that he wanted to help and was committed to both endeavors, but needed to pare back his involvements for the sake of his health and family.

To George's surprise, everyone was OK with the limits he set. No one was mad at him or disappointed in his efforts. In fact, they commended him for being honest with them and thanked him for his work. Saying no will never come easily to George, but it gets easier every time, and he is happier and healthier for it.

DIMINISH

Does the term *shortcut* have a negative connotation for you? Have you ever considered why? Most people say, "Well, by the time I figure out the shortcut, I could've finished the job already." And that's true, especially if you're talking about a task that takes fifteen minutes. But maybe you're reluctant for a completely different reason. Does "taking a shortcut" take you back to the times you prayed you wouldn't get caught while dashing across the neighborhood Boo Radley's backyard? Or perhaps a parent, favorite teacher, or coach taught you to believe that shortcuts are "the easy way out," that you'd never see results if you didn't put in the time. Do you feel guilty or like a cheat trying to find a less complicated or faster way through something?

When you're used to doing things a certain way, or are committed to doing everything you do perfectly, then diminishing any task, no matter how trivial, can feel like a cop-out. How do you make the leap from keeping a meticulously detailed checkbook to banking on-line? Or from meeting every prospective client for lunch to simply scheduling a conference call? It can be difficult to conquer that need for perfection; after all, the intention behind your efforts is well-meaning. Training yourself out of your perfectionist tendencies can feel unnatural.

Wanting to present your absolute best self on everything you do is an admirable quality. But it's impossible to do everything perfectly, at home or at the office. And taking shortcuts isn't cheating or finding the easy way out; it's being as efficient as the situation demands. Remember, in most instances it's far better to have something completed (even if it's less than perfect) than not done at all. Sometimes good enough is good enough.

Let's say you have to write an extremely important memo, on a very tight deadline. Your boss races in around 2 p.m. and says, "Hey, can you put something together for the CEO? He needs to take it with him on a five-thirty p.m. flight. He just set up a meeting with a prospective investor." Your instinctive response is, "Sure, of course." But now what?

You know that to do this right, you need several hours. Your normal process is to start from scratch, root through market research, gather backup materials, outline the main points, draft the memo, run it by your boss for approval, and then polish it. But there isn't enough time. This situation demands a shortcut. Using a previously prepared memo as a template, you doctor it for this prospective client. You grab a packet you did for someone else last week and begin to adapt it. You keep the body essentially the same (after all, that was approved by your boss last week) and throw the bulk of your effort into drafting killer first and last paragraphs until they really sing. You shuffle through the backup promotional material, pull out two items that don't relate to this client, and shove in three that are related to the new prospect's industry.

In under two hours, you have assembled a perfectly acceptable packet that will do the job (even though you know it could've been better if you had more time). The important thing is that the job is done, the CEO has the packet in time to review on the plane, and your boss is pleased.

Learning how to diminish tasks at home is equally important (and tough to do).

GETTING REAL

Charlotte, Picture Perfect

Charlotte had worked for several years as a fashion photographer. She preferred to develop all of her own film, even after she left the fashion world and her primary subjects were her own children. But it was so hard to keep up. Eventually she stopped documenting her kids' lives in pictures altogether because she couldn't do it perfectly. Charlotte felt guilty and was frustrated with herself, but what could she do? Photography had been her livelihood. How could she do a half-baked job?

I suggested that having some pictures was better than having none at all. A digital camera would make it easy to capture memories, plus it eliminated the developing process completely. Charlotte occasionally did take some family photos with her old equipment and develop the film herself, but only on really special occasions, like birthdays and graduations.

Sometimes the process (how you get there) is just as important as the result, but most of the time, the outcome is what really counts. For more specifics on diminishing tasks, or finding shortcuts, see chapter 4, "The WADE Formula."

DELEGATE TASKS

Let's say you've determined that a task absolutely must be carried out, and you've streamlined it so that it will take the least amount of time possible. The next question is whether you have to do it yourself, or whether you can purge it from your schedule by delegating it to someone else. When you authorize others to take over some of your activities, you free yourself to focus your time and efforts on those tasks where you can make your best contribution.

One of the most delightful aspects of delegating is that it promotes a very healthy interdependence among people. Working as a team brings people together. Relationships solidify as you share the workload and learn to rely on one another.

Although delegation is one of the most powerful tools for effective time management, it's also the most psychologically loaded. Relying on others brings up deep-seated issues of dependency and trust. If you feel guilty asking for help, are wary of being expendable, have extremely high standards, or are generally mistrusting, sharing the workload is a challenge. Does the following sound familiar?

- **You feel too busy to delegate.** When you are overwhelmed with things to do, it can feel like you don't have the time to invest in delegating and supervising someone else. However, investing a few hours or even minutes figuring out what you can delegate, finding someone to help, and training him or her can save you enormous amounts of time. Don't be afraid to take time out to formulate a plan.

- **You feel guilty "dumping" on others.** If you think of delegation as giving someone else the undesirable or grunt work, you may feel guilty doing it. After all, none of us wants to be the big bad boss. Then again, you don't have to martyr yourself! Just because you don't like doing a task doesn't mean someone else won't enjoy it. Yes, some tasks and projects aren't "fun" or "fantastic learning experiences," but that's life, and that's work; someone is getting paid to do that work! We all have different skills, interests, and talents, so don't feel guilty asking someone else to help. Delegation works best when you put the right person in the right job at the right time and allow everyone to make an important contribution to the success of a goal.

- **You have difficulty depending on others.** Some people are imprisoned by an "If I don't do this myself, it won't get done right" mentality. If you grew up in an environment where you couldn't depend on the people around you, it will be especially hard for you to depend on others.

  Think of delegating as an opportunity for personal growth. If you've never really relied on others, you're in for a happy surprise—other people can bring fresh and wonderful ideas to a task you're stuck on. Focus on the fact that like you, most people are responsible and intelligent and like to make a contribution.

- **You're afraid of becoming dispensable.** You may resist delegating because you are afraid that if someone else can do your job, you will no longer be needed or have value. If you really thought about it, you would probably see that other people's need for you is not tied up in just one task or your ability to handle several tasks at once. You have a reserve of unique skills, ideas, and personal traits that make you valuable to others. So let go of tasks that other people can do and free yourself for new projects.

Who Is the Best Person for the Job?

As you're deciding to whom to delegate, keep in mind that there are three kinds of delegatees, each requiring a different investment of your time.

- **Delegate to an expert.** Giving the job to someone who can do it better, faster, or more efficiently than you requires the least investment of time on your part and provides an almost instant time-savings. Get your teenager to program your new cell phone—it'll take him fifteen minutes compared to your two hours! Or hire a handyman to install the bookshelves. His knowledge of how to find studs in the wall and hang shelves level will save you hours of tapping.
- **Delegate to an equal.** Giving the job to someone who is just as qualified as you also reduces the amount of explaining time and makes it pretty likely that the task will be done just fine. If you give laundry duties to your spouse, your shirts may not be creased exactly as you like them, but the clothes will be just as clean. And it'll free your time to tend to more important things on your agenda.
- **Delegate to a beginner.** Giving the job to someone who's not as skilled as you is a leap of faith! It requires more of your time, as you will have to train and supervise, but offers great rewards. You become a mentor and may earn yourself a grateful helper (who's happy for the opportunity to learn!). At home, give your kids the responsibility of tending to the vegetable garden. It

might take a few weeks for them to get the hang of weeding and learn the dangers of overwatering, but in a month or so, you'll be able to reclaim a few hours each week, and they can be responsible for making the salad every night! At work, consider delegating some of your creative work (like writing copy for the Web site) to your assistant. After the initial investment of time, it'll feel good to have upped his or her confidence, and it may inspire you to find other projects he or she can help with.

Who knows? Your helper's approach may teach you a thing or two!

Your goal is to assign each person to the job in which he or she can make the best possible contribution to the project. Consider your team members' talents, skills, vision, and availability. As you look over each task that needs to be done, ask yourself:

- Who is good at this?
- Who might enjoy this, or at least certain parts of this?
- Who might want to learn about this?
- Who is available?

Exercise: What Would You Like to Delegate? And to Whom?

Task	To Whom?
_____	_____
_____	_____
_____	_____
_____	_____

Keep Your Delegation Options Open

Don't limit yourself to the obvious candidates! At home, your team includes all your family members. But if there are tasks that extend beyond the availability or talents of your family, enlist others. Take advantage of delivery services. Hire a housekeeper or gardener, or a local kid to run errands. If you can't afford to hire help, try bartering with friends and neighbors. Some neighborhoods have created cooking co-ops that save all the members a lot of work while building community.

The same holds true in the workplace. A common mistake managers make is that they often limit themselves to their staff, when in some cases getting an outside consultant or contractor would be more efficient and cost-effective.

GETTING REAL

Maureen, Working Mom

Maureen, married to her second husband, had two children from her first marriage. A marketing executive at a national bank, her work life was smooth and easy compared to her home life. Buzzing and jolting from one task to the next, she was in constant motion and spent almost no quality time with her husband or kids.

As she described the flow of her week, I was struck by how much responsibility she carried on her shoulders. Every morning, she work, dressed, fed, and chauffeured her kids to school. Every night after she came home from work, she'd pick up the clutter, wash the floor, prepare dinner, serve it, and clean up while her kids did their homework. On the weekends she did all the food-shopping, errand-running, and laundry.

Whenever I tell this story at a seminar the people in the audience cut in at this point, shrieking, "Where is her husband? Get that guy to do something!" Fair point.

But the first thing I actually asked Maureen was, "Why do you wash the floor every night?" Looking a little surprised by my question, Maureen shrugged. "Well, that's what my mother always did." I asked, "Did your mother work?" Long pause. "Ummm, no, actually, she didn't." So on top of being one of the family's breadwinners, she was burdening herself with work that was more befitting of a fifties stay-at-home mom—and it was taking its toll.

It wasn't that her husband and children refused to help. In fact, they'd tried repeatedly to pitch in. Maureen was so focused on taking full responsibility for the kids (since they were her kids from her first marriage, she didn't feel it was fair to burden her second husband) and on doing things a certain way that she made it nearly impossible for anyone to contribute. The house was organized in a way that made everyone completely dependent on her. In touring the pantry, I noticed that the healthy snack foods and cereals were all on a high shelf, so that if the kids were hungry, they'd have to ask her to get something down for them. I asked why she wouldn't let her husband clean up after dinner. "Well, he offers, but he never puts the things back in the right cabinet."

The solutions were simple. Labeling the shelves in the kitchen would ensure that whoever put the dishes away put them in the right cabinet. By moving the kids' snack food from a high shelf to a lower one, they could help themselves. I suggested other ways to share the workload. The kids could pick out their clothes the night before and get themselves dressed in time for breakfast. If they all picked the clutter up on time, they could play a game before leaving for school. They could cook dinner as a family. After dinner, she and Bob could clean up while the kids did their homework. We posted a shopping list on the fridge where items could be checked off on an as-needed basis, and Bob could take the kids shopping on the weekend while Maureen went to the gym.

The hardest part was getting Maureen to give up the fantasy of herself as a fifties stay-at-home mom (with a full-time executive job). Delegating chores didn't make her less of a mom or wife—it actually made her more accessible to her family. As the family relaxed and did chores together, they got closer and Maureen was convinced she'd done the right thing. The one task she had the easiest time giving up? Washing the floor every night. She relinquished that in a New York minute.

DELAY

Delaying tasks can also have a negative connotation if you grew up with a parent whose favorite aphorism went something like: "Don't put off for tomorrow what you can do today." While that expression holds some truth, it was written many decades ago, when life was simpler and there weren't so many things that you *could* do on any given day. Delaying does not have to mean that you are procrastinating; you are simply postponing the task or activity to a time that works better with your schedule and priorities. Delaying in this sense is actually *proactive*—you are choosing the best time to do something instead of just shoving it into the moment.

In this opportunity-rich world, delaying a task often involves postponing our own gratification. Just as you are preparing to gather your papers for tax time, a friend calls to invite you to the movies. You'd so rather go see a film, but it'd be wiser to delay your outing with your friend for the evening and stick to the task at hand—so that you are prepared for your accountant on Monday.

Or, you're cleaning up your house for a party and get the urge to switch your closets from winter to spring. You already have a full list of party-preparations to-do. As gratifying as it might be to change over your closet, it's a task that you should delay, to keep your day calm and avoid jamming yourself at the last minute.

When looking at your list of to-dos, ask yourself what can really wait. What absolutely doesn't have to happen today. And reschedule those items to different days so that you can create a realistic, enjoyable plan for the day.

Learning to let go, whether that means deleting, delegating, diminishing, or delaying, isn't easy, especially if you want to do it all. But staying connected to your big-picture goals can make it easier. There are only so many hours in the day. Remind yourself that if you try to do everything, something, somewhere will get short shrift.

In the next chapter, "Assign," you'll learn how and when to schedule the tasks you choose to do into your days.

13

ASSIGN A HOME

Now that you have decided what you are going to do, you need to be specific about when you will do things. It's time to assign a "home," a specific time in your day or week for each of the tasks you have decided to do.

Assigning a home is done in conjunction with your planner—you must record all of your to-dos directly into your planner on the day you intend to do them. The questions to yourself are, "When am I going to do the task?" "Will I do it this week or next? Today or tomorrow?"

Why not leave timing to chance? Here's the bottom line: A "to-do" not connected to a "when" rarely gets done. There are so many distractions and demands on our time that if you don't carve out the specific day and time to do what's most important to you, twenty other things will fill that space. Tying your "to-do" to a "when" leaves you free to focus on each moment, assured that there is time enough for all you need to do.

PROACTIVE VS. REACTIVE

You may be thinking: "Sure, this is all very sensible in theory, but I live in the real world. I can't dictate when I do everything. I get demands and requests from people who want things done on their timetable. There's no way to know when a crisis or interruption is going to happen." To some extent this is true; you can't *always* have it your way. The key to assigning a home is to recognize that in most cases you do have the power to decide when.

Too often you feel like a victim, reacting instantly to every demand or idea that comes your way. This knee-jerk reaction is the result of getting caught up in other people's priorities and not having a master plan of your own. Without a "place" to funnel tasks, you feel that if you don't do something immediately, you might never get to it, so you do it right away.

If you're always in a reactive mode, you'll not only feel out of control, you'll lose time and productivity. Assigning a home puts you back in command. You can often postpone dealing with certain tasks until you are ready and that always saves time because you approach the task when you are best prepared to tackle it.

Assigning a specific home counteracts the lack of productivity that results if you do things only when you are "in the mood." The fact is that you may never be in the mood for many of the tasks on your list. Are you ever really in the mood to go to the dentist, pay your bills, or write up an expense report?

Finally, assigning a home instantly alerts you if this task is going to throw off your balance. Let's say you have designated three hours to run errands and have lunch with a friend on Saturday, but when you add up the time you realize the entire outing will take you four hours. You could choose to spend four hours with your friend, but that means cutting into the hour of your afternoon that you've already allotted for an outing with your child. So, instead you eliminate or shorten one task and assign it to another day.

CREATE START AND STOP TIMES

Some people feel confined when they schedule everything down to the smallest increment of time, while others feel more confident that they will stay on track if they know what they are doing in any given half-hour time block. Your agenda should be firm enough to provide a structure that enables you to achieve your goals, but flexible enough to bend and sway with the realities of your life.

If you thrive on a lot of structure, you may always want to assign a specific time to each phone call (10 a.m.), task (10:20–11 a.m.), and project (12–2:30 p.m.). If you prefer flexibility, you might simply want to say, "I'll make phone calls from nine to eleven a.m. These are the eight calls I want to make and I'll do them in whatever order feels good at the time."

Assigning a specific time limit and deadline for each task has several benefits.

1. When you're particularly busy and you have a ton of stuff to fit in, assigning a specific time to each task helps you stay on track and moving forward.

2. It forces you to place a relative value on each task: How much time do you really want to spend on it? How much time do you need to think, and play, and make decisions? I've found that tasks often expand into the time you allot them. If you give yourself an hour to do something, you'll use the full hour. The reverse is also true, especially when it comes to tasks you despise doing. What if you only gave yourself thirty minutes to do your expense reports instead of a full hour? Would you be able to do it? Of course, and in half the time!

Tuesday • September 5

SEPTEMBER

S	M	T	W	T	F	S
					1	2
3	4	5	6	7	8	9
10	11	12	13	14	15	16
17	18	19	20	21	22	23
24	25	26	27	28	29	30

AUGUST

S	M	T	W	T	F	S
		1	2	3	4	5
6	7	8	9	10	11	12
13	14	15	16	17	18	19
20	21	22	23	24	25	26
27	28	29	30	31		

OCTOBER

S	M	T	W	T	F	S
1	2	3	4	5	6	7
8	9	10	11	12	13	14
15	16	17	18	19	20	21
22	23	24	25	26	27	28
29	30	31				

TO DO

TO DO

Absolutely DON'T forget

early am

8 _SELF—Wake up, make coffee, check e-mail._

9 _FAMILY— Breakfast and shower routine with husband and baby._

10 _FAMILY/WORK— Phone call to cowriter/cleaning kitchen. Husband takes baby for day._

11 _HOME— Neighborhood errands—grocery store, dry cleaners, drugstore. Put away_

12 _groceries, laundry and pur- chases, file receipts, check in with husband._

1 _SELF— Lunch. Bike ride._

2 _FAMILY/FRIEND— Take care of baby for a few hours while straightening up and/or making personal_

3 _calls._

4

5 _FAMILY— Dinner prep, eating, and cleanup._

6 _FAMILY— Pick up clutter and start hand washing._

7 _FAMILY— Watch movie with hus- band, hand-washing, playing with baby._

8

9 _FAMILY— Put baby to bed. Relationship Time._

10 _Time with husband. SELF— Journal writing. Bed._

late pm

A home weekend to-do list. I've noted here the categories for all these tasks, but you don't need to do this when making out your own list.

February
24 HOUR SCHEDULE

FEBRUARY						
S	M	T	W	T	F	S
		1	2	3	4	5
6	7	8	9	10	11	12
13	14	15	16	17	18	19
20	21	22	23	24	25	26
27	28	29				

7 AM
CLIENT MATTERS —
   Smith case

7 PM

8

8

9 COMMUTE — proof -
   reading

9
*Calls to make —
   Blahno

10
OPEN — calls*

10 Marvin
   Kathy R.
   Tax commissioner

11
CLIENT MATTERS —
   Jones Case

11

12 NOON
LUNCH — Working
   at desk*

12 MIDNIGHT
*e-mail —
   Respond to Bill Z.

1
MEETING W/CLIENTS
   · Ward

1 Soap Company
   Stats to Maura R.
   Sanders's Comptroller

2
   · Shapiro

2

3 CLIENT MATTERS —
   Wells case

3

4 OPEN — calls*

4

5

5

6 COMMUTE — reading
   professional journal

A lawyer's work to-do list. Note that the list of calls and e-mails for the day are in the right column; these will be made during one of the three time slots for calls and e-mails.

WHAT SIZE IS THE SANDBOX?

For certain tasks, it's extremely helpful to know how much time, ideally, you should allot for it. It's not so little time that you feel constricted and tense, and not so much time that you feel like the task is going to go on forever and consume you. This is especially true of difficult tasks that we tend to procrastinate on—writing, bill paying, cleaning, and assembling tax papers. If you find the right size sandbox for the task, you'll get it done and circumvent procrastination entirely.

Let's say you have to pay bills, and you've decided to do it on Saturday. If you sit down thinking, "I'm just going to work on these bills until they are done," the task may seem to stretch endlessly before you. But if you say, "I'm going to get these bills done in half an hour," it suddenly seems short-lived enough to get you started. Turn to Saturday, write "Pay Bills 11:00–11:30." Then schedule something wonderful for immediately after. The perfect-sized sandbox.

GETTING REAL

Julie's Writing Sandbox

When I first began writing, I had no idea how much time I needed to get anything done. Whether I was drafting an article, outlining a book chapter, or composing promotional copy, I didn't know how much time to set aside for the task. Two hours was not enough for me to relax into my thoughts and make any progress. Scheduling all day was too much. What could I do for all that time? I began asking other writers how much time they spent at their computers, really focused, every day. Most could generate highly creative thoughts for about three to four hours. So, I tried adjusting my sandbox, and began scheduling all writing tasks into a four-hour window. I'd start early in the morning, so that I'd still have time for other professional commitments later in the day. It worked. Three or four hours was just enough time for me to relax into my thoughts, follow an idea through, and come to a satisfying point of completion.

Some days the words flow for four hours. Other days it takes me a while to warm up and I may only write for two hours of my assigned writing time. But with a four-hour sandbox, I'm usually able to accomplish what I need to for the day before moving on to my next project.

I call that your personal sandbox—the particular amount of time that makes you most comfortable embarking on a task.

Exercise: Think About the Following Tasks
What sized sandbox is right for you?

Pay bills?   _____

Clean the dishes?   _____

Assemble expense reports?   _____

Clean the house?   _____

Write a thank-you note?   _____

Write a letter?   _____

ARRANGING YOUR DAY

There are two basic strategies to planning out your day: (1) honoring your Time Map or (2) going according to your own natural rhythms. Use whichever method works best with your situation and personality. Let's start with your natural rhythms first.

There are some roles, jobs, and personalities that operate on a running-list basis. If you are a support person (assistant, customer service rep, stock broker) or a crisis manager, you probably need to address tasks and issues as soon as they come to you. Often these tasks are quick hits: Call Bill, mail this, fax that, deal with this fire, watch out for that problem.

Exceptionally free-spirited people who thrive on spontaneity might balk at the idea of committing themselves to doing something on a specific day or at a specific time. You still need to decide, at least generally, which day of the week you are going to do things. With no plan whatsoever, how will you ever get anything done? There's a difference between being flexible and spontaneous, and being completely vague. If you at least have an idea of which day or week you'll get to something (even if it's not set in stone), you are positioning yourself for being proactive, and (how about this?) actually getting the task done.

Strategy #1: Follow Your Natural Rhythms

If you've opted for something less formal than a traditional Time Map to keep in balance, you still need to decide *when* you are going to do something. Experiment with different ways of grouping your tasks. You may hit upon a rhythm that inspires you to be your most productive. The important thing is to lay out your tasks in a way that feels natural to you. Use the factors below to help guide your decisions:

- **Urgency:** Make the activity with the earliest and most pressing due date your top priority. If you have an important memo due at work, or a mortgage application to submit, flag it as an urgent task. Even if you end up with plenty of time to accomplish everything on your list, getting the most critical task or two done first will fuel you with a sense of accomplishment and the energy to keep going.

- **Variety:** Vary your activities to keep your energy high and yourself engaged. If you've been reading for three hours, and your eyes are starting to cross, switch things up. You may find it easier to stay focused if you do something more active, like making a phone call or grabbing coffee with a coworker.

  Your social life can also benefit from an occasional change of pace. Having a core group you spend your time with is comfortable and fun, but expanding your social circle can keep your horizons broad, expose you to new ideas, and make you feel a little less dependent on your group.

- **Duration.** If you only have thirty minutes, use the time to do a task you know you can get done (e.g., make two phone calls or read an article), rather than try to tackle a great big task that will require at least a couple of hours (e.g., writing copy for the Web site).

  When other people are involved, remember to figure in prep time, travel time, and cleanup time, and then schedule accordingly. When in doubt, tack on twenty minutes as a cushion.

- **Significance:** During each block of time, ask yourself which assignment you would love to cross off your list. This is hardly ever your easiest task. It might even be the most difficult. Whatever task will give you the greatest sense of relief and satisfaction to have completed is the one you should do first.

  Choose activities and people that will support and enhance your big-picture goals. If one pal at work is always pressuring you into social situations, figure out a polite way to duck out the next time she tries to drag you to an event. It's important to be true to yourself, so that your social life is an extension of, rather than a distraction from, your interests.

- **Energy or Interest Level.** We all have natural energy cycles and moments when we can concentrate better than others. Select a task that matches your energy level to make the most out of the time available. Always try to do your toughest tasks when you're at your peak energy level—they'll be much easier then. When it comes to your social life, some friends and events are so comfortable and enjoyable, they actually give you energy, so it doesn't matter how tired you are when you get together. Others require more effort, so be sure to check your energy before saying yes. Also, consider how interested you are in the proposed activity. If you always end up going to the movies, even though you really want to attend a poetry reading, speak up! Who knows? Your friends might be bored of the same-old, same-old routine, too.
- **Geography.** If you are running errands, you could run the mall errands and then all the errands that require travel to the other side of town.

Strategy #2: Follow Your Time Map, If You Have One

If you have chosen to use a traditional Time Map, your goal will be to funnel every task into its predetermined zone. For example, let's say that one of the major categories of your work is Development, and you've blocked out time for development-related activities every day from 11 a.m. to 1 p.m. Say you're working out the budget for a new event during this time slot when you suddenly remember that you're supposed to e-mail your boss details about a problematic client. Should you stop to do it right then? (Surely it's important—your boss needs that information.) Wrong answer! Instead, open your planner or whip out your PalmPilot and check if there's enough time available in your "client" zone later that afternoon. If there is, simply pencil in "Write client memo." If not, decide if it can wait until tomorrow (when there is room), or if it's important enough to bump one of your other tasks. It's as simple as that.

MAINTAINING BALANCE WITH TRADE-OFFS

Of course, there will be times when you just can't funnel a task into the correct activity zone on your Time Map. For example, let's say an old friend is in town on business. Typically you use Tuesday evenings for "Family Errands" but your buddy will only be in town Tuesday and Wednesday—and you really want to see her. Do you tell your friend, "Sorry, I can't go to dinner because it's 'family errand' night"? Of course not! You make a trade-off.

To find another time in your week to get those errands done, take a look at your Time Map. Let's say Saturday afternoon is your "Self" time—there's your answer! That week, just swap Tuesday night for Saturday afternoon. Making that even trade ensures that you cover all your bases.

If an exact substitution isn't possible, try juggling your schedule. For example, if you can't run errands on Saturday afternoon because you already have something planned, see if someone else in your family can do it or if you can put it off until next week. If those errands absolutely must be done, sacrifice something else, but make sure you schedule extra time to make up for it the following week.

You have a lot of flexibility when you work with your Time Map. The most important thing is to be aware of the trade-offs you are making and always strive to regain the balance you have set for yourself.

HONOR THE DECISIONS YOU HAVE MADE

Think of the time you've blocked out for your to-dos as if they were appointments with real people. That means not rushing to cancel them when something else comes up.

At the office, you need to communicate when you are unavailable because you already have other work scheduled. Tell people, "I'm sorry, I have an appointment." They don't need to know it's an appointment with yourself to get a project done for a couple of hours, or to go work out. Presumably you've appropriately prioritized your to-dos and the work you're doing at any given moment is important. If your boss is the person who's requesting you to make a different task priority number one, explain what you're working on and let him help you decide whether you should continue what you're doing or drop it and switch to something else.

The same goes with activities and chores you have planned at home. You made a conscious decision to include these things in your schedule because they are essential to who you are and they're helping you achieve your big-picture goals. So don't give them up! Honor the hard work and thought you have poured into this process so far by keeping your appointments with you.

When your day is laid out like this, and you have the right amount of time to get things done, it's very gratifying. Instead of being defeated by your to-do list, you can claim victory. You can look at your list and think, "Wow! I've got enough time to do this!" What's more, you get to determine how much time you'll allow for paying the bills, or working out, or writing a proposal, or reading the paper. You can allot as much or as little time as feels comfortable to you. It feels wonderful. It's empowering!

We've spent a lot of time deciding which activities you want to do and when you want to do them. It's important to stick to your plan, which means starting and stopping when you plan to. How do you do this? By learning to "containerize" tasks, that is, by preventing one task from spilling over into the time allotted for the next. In the next chapter, you'll do battle with the biggest enemies to your schedule: procrastination, chronic lateness, and interruptions.

14

CONTAINERIZE

Plan your work, and then work your plan.

Containerizing is a critical skill that all the best time managers have mastered. They make swift decisions. They don't procrastinate. They are rarely late. They do exactly what they plan to do, when they plan to do it, with little hesitation. Because they get their to-dos done in the time they have allotted for them, they move through their days feeling energized, optimistic, and satisfied.

So how do you containerize time? In three ways:

1. Conquering procrastination
2. Overcoming chronic lateness
3. Minimizing interruptions and their impact

In my experience, once people have gotten to the "containerize" stage of this process, most self-sabotaging behavior has disappeared on its own. Since you have built your schedule from the inside out, your day is now filled with activities that energize you, and you see the connection between everything you are doing and your big-picture goals. You feel inspired and motivated to begin each day and are excited about moving from one task on your list to the next. You have a higher appreciation of the value of your time and are less likely to squander it.

However, you may still periodically find yourself up against some of the following challenges. Let's see what's behind them and learn techniques to overcome them.

CONQUERING PROCRASTINATION

Procrastination is the biggest enemy of a successfully planned day. When you get a late start, one activity spills over into the time allotted for the next, causing a domino effect that leaves many items on your to-do list undone. You compound the problem when you procrastinate by puttering around on totally meaningless tasks, tasks that are not connected to your goals. In this worst-case scenario, time spent procrastinating is truly a waste. One of the worst effects of procrastination is the energy drain that results. You spend a lot of time beating yourself up for not accomplishing what you need to accomplish, and this steals even more time and energy from your ability to move on to the next thing on your to-do list.

There are many causes for procrastination. Fortunately, many of them are simple to fix. First, ask yourself whether you procrastinate on only some tasks or on practically everything.

- If you procrastinate on *only some tasks,* the cause is probably technical. There is something about the way you are approaching those tasks that has you at a standstill. You may need to learn to break the task down into smaller components or think of that one type of task differently. The tips below will help you get unstuck.
- If you procrastinate *about everything,* it's likely that your motives are psychologically based. Read the section on lateness below

and refer to chapter 2, "What's Holding You Back?" paying particular attention to the issues of Fear of Failure or Success, Fear of Completion, and Conquistador of Chaos.

In either case, the tips below may help you get unstuck.

- **Trust your instincts.** In many ways procrastination is simply about putting off decisions. Making swift decisions is essential to completing projects and staying on schedule. So how do you make good decisions quickly? By trusting your instincts.
- **Focus on your goal.** When you keep your eye on the benefits of the task, rather than on the dreaded task itself, it can make any process more tolerable. Recognize that each task is only one aspect of a larger plan and that no one decision is going to make or break your success. It's a very liberating realization, and it makes it easier to move quickly through the decisions you have to make. If you make a decision quickly, you will then have time to do a reality check on how that decision feels.
- **Do a different step.** Sometimes, you procrastinate because you really aren't ready to move ahead. You may not have all the information you need to make a decision yet, or you may not be prepared for the outcome the project will produce. For example, you may be procrastinating about hiring a new employee because you aren't really ready to commit to another salary right now. You may be procrastinating on purchasing a new camera because you feel you are lacking certain skills to master how to use it. If you aren't ready to tackle a particular task, what you can do is focus your efforts on steps that will get you ready. If you are putting off hiring an assistant because you aren't ready for the additional expense, your next step could be to reanalyze your profit margin or add another revenue stream. If you are postponing that proposal because of a skill you lack, try taking a course or reading up on that skill as your next step.

- **Break down overwhelming tasks into manageable parts.** Instead of facing one huge, amorphous task, divide it into three (or six, or ten) achievable steps. Each step could be one hour or one day in duration. Then concentrate on only the first step.

- **Combine a miserable task with something you enjoy.** What if it's a task you can't delegate, such as exercising or going to the dentist? Try combining it with something you absolutely love to do. If you hate to exercise, read while walking on a treadmill, go to the gym with a friend whose company you love, or go in-line skating with your kids. Or bribe yourself: Schedule a manicure immediately following every dentist's appointment. Read a junk magazine (the kind you are embarrassed to enjoy) whenever you go to the dentist—and only when you go to the dentist.

- **Give yourself a time limit.** You can always give your task a very short time limit. Just get started. Knowing the torture won't go on forever will help you to stop procrastinating. You may even be encouraged to continue the job past your time limit. Once you are in motion, everything changes. You are engaged and connected. You feel the wind in your face and you feel better about yourself. You'll be surprised how your energy and momentum build. Before you know it, you will be enjoying the journey.

- **Impose your own deadline.** Many people really do work better under pressure. When they're working with a deadline hanging over them, they are freed from a certain level of perfectionism, which permits them to lighten up, stop worrying, and just do it.

  If leaving everything to the last minute truly helps you perform better, the first step is to accept this about yourself. Then establish self-imposed deadlines in advance of the actual deadline. If you have a proposal due on Friday, make your deadline three days earlier. Then book other urgent matters in the days following the proposal. This keeps you under pressure but builds in a three-day cushion in case anything really goes wrong. You'll be safe.

In my experience, most people who adopt this "false deadline" technique eventually outgrow the need to do things at the last minute. After a while, they discover how liberating it is to have things done a few days in advance and then they begin to enjoy getting things done ahead of time.

- **Adopt a catchphrase.** Sometimes, adopting a phrase or ditty to motivate yourself to just get started may be all you need: "Just do it." "Do it now!" "If not now, when?" I think of a Mr. Rogers song, "You've got to do it, just do it." I heard it one day while watching the show with my daughter when she was little. It's very simple and is just what I need to get me past any moments of hesitation.

OVERCOMING CHRONIC LATENESS

Chronic lateness will throw your schedule off just as much as procrastination will. Lateness is an emotionally charged issue. What's fascinating is how people on both sides of the issue have so little understanding of the other party's experience. The perfectly punctual are convinced that lateness is a blatantly rude act of arrogance, one that implies, "My time is more important than yours." They see lateness as deliberate, hostile, and easily curable—*Just leave a few minutes earlier, okay?*

The majority of the perpetually tardy are lost in their own emotional turmoil. Their lives are filled with harried moments, near misses, and guilty apologies. They're just so immersed in their own chaos that they rarely realize how inconsiderate their behavior appears to the people left waiting. They think everyone struggles with this problem.

Pinpoint the Problem

In order to diagnose what's going on, you need to ask yourself, "Am I always late by *different* amounts of time or am I always late by the *same* amount of time?"

- If you are always late by *different amounts of time* (i.e., sometimes five minutes late, sometimes twenty-five minutes late), the problem is likely to be purely technical. You probably need to brush up on your time-estimating skills (see chapter 3, "Making Time Tangible") or your ability to say no (see chapter 12, "Purge") or a propensity to get sidetracked by interruptions, which ruin your own plans. The third section of this chapter offers tips for controlling interruptions.
- Always late by the *same amount of time?* It's more likely that the issue has psychological roots. After all, if you're always exactly late by fifteen minutes, you are obviously showing up exactly when you want to. The question becomes, Why do you want to be late?

Sometimes punctuality is simply a matter of regional or cultural differences. A New Orleans native now living in the Northeast confesses she is late for practically everything. But she also doesn't mind when other people show up past the scheduled meeting time. In the South, no one is on time! When she's left waiting for others, she simply reads a book and relaxes.

Sure, some people are on a power trip and like to arrive last to make a grand entrance, but they are more the exception than the rule. Chronic lateness is more often the result of Fear of Downtime or being a Conquistador of Chaos, two issues introduced in chapter 2, "What's Holding You Back?"

Because this is such a big issue, let's explore it a little further here.

GETTING REAL

Natalie, Chronically Late

Natalie has been late her whole life. As a kid, she never made it to school on time, even though her elementary school was just down the block. At fifty-six, happily married, with two grown children and a successful career, she is still late for work every day. Natalie crams every moment with activity—going to the gym six times a week, lunching with friends, attending dinner parties, and racing to business meetings, weekend brunches, movies, and museums. She's late for them all.

Friends tell her she has no sense of how long things take. She's tried to be more conscious, more sensitive, and makes a big effort to give herself extra time. But she always gets caught up in the feeling of *I've got to fit one more thing in.*

Her mornings start off the same every day. The alarm sounds at 6:00 a.m., then sounds again at ten-minute intervals until Natalie finally rouses at 6:40. She takes a shower, enjoys breakfast while reading the paper, and aims to leave the house by 7:30, mindful that it takes a solid thirty minutes to get to work. She runs upstairs for some last-minute prep, and by the time she's clutching her car keys, it's 7:35 a.m.

Now it's panic time. Having denied how long her morning ritual takes until she's actually on her way, Natalie is suddenly miserably aware of reality. Once she's in her car, the dashboard clock mocks her. The slightest bit of traffic sends her blood racing. Her daily thirty-minute commute has become, once again, an anxiety-ridden journey of dread, self-recrimination, and nagging worry. She rushes into her office at 8:10, and the tone has been set for her whole workday.

Natalie has a vague notion that her rushing, never-on-time style has something to do with avoidance. Avoidance of thinking? Avoidance of something having to do with strong, painful emotions? She isn't sure. Attempting to fix the lateness issue often means dealing with whatever lies beneath it—the kind of stuff we typically spend our whole lives in therapy trying to get to . . . or avoid.

I was hesitant to probe Natalie too deeply (I'm not a psychologist). Still, many of us lead suspiciously busy lives. Fear of downtime—near-panic at the thought of a day or an evening off, or two weeks away from work—is immensely common.

I pointed out to Natalie that she obviously enjoys her downtime; it was the fact that she was sleeping a little longer in the morning and savoring the paper before exiting the house that made her late everyday. Why not give herself permission to enjoy additional relaxed moments throughout the day? How? By leaving on time and getting to places with time to spare.

We came up with two strategies. The first was purely pragmatic: Counting backward together, we calculated that if she awoke ten minutes earlier and left for work at 7:20 instead of 7:30, she could enjoy that second cup of coffee and not have to feel rushed. My second suggestion was simply emotional food for thought. When Natalie *did* arrive someplace early, I encouraged her to become more mindful of her emotional reflexes, and perhaps take the first tentative steps toward acknowledging whatever feelings came up.

Two weeks later, Natalie proudly reported that she'd been two to five minutes early for work almost every day since our conversation, and it felt, well, great to be on time. The one day she got there two minutes late, she was actually mad at herself.

Did she have an opportunity to reflect on her anxiety, I asked? Yes! Meeting a friend for lunch early one afternoon, Natalie showed up at the restaurant five minutes early, and her friend arrived five minutes late. Natalie had ten full minutes of . . . waiting. The thoughts and feelings flooding her mind were *What if I got the time wrong? What if she forgot we're meeting? What if something happened and she doesn't show up and I'm left to my own resources? What will I do?* Unused to doing things alone, Natalie was aware mostly of feeling afraid—of being disconnected from people.

It was less important for our work to understand the exact roots of her fear than to accept the reality and give her a practical strategy. Over the next week, I recommended that Natalie schedule activities that would make her feel connected while she waited. Reading a book might not do the trick (too solitary), but reviewing her appointments for the week ahead, writing a thank-you note, or making a phone call might satisfy her desire for companionship just perfectly.

Weeks later, I checked in with Natalie, and she'd been able to sustain this new on-time approach. She sounded like a new woman, no longer afraid to be on time, enjoying her more relaxed, nonapologetic state. Natalie had broken through to the other side.

Respect Your Anxiety

If you find the idea of getting places early and waiting fills you with dread, *respect that feeling*. We tend to minimize lateness, treating it as nothing more than a bad habit, when indeed it can be a symptom, an indicator, a gateway, an opportunity to learn more about ourselves. Natalie was able to solve her issues by identifying and overcoming a gnawing and irrational worry that her friends, companions, and colleagues would forget her. Whatever the roots of your anxiety, you can conquer chronic lateness with some of the following suggestions:

- **Improve your time estimating skills.** Brush up on your skills at honestly calculating how long things take, using the techniques in chapter 3. You're probably only off by about ten minutes, so timing your routines and accepting them will be the first step. Until you get better at estimating how long tasks take, build in a cushion of time for yourself before appointments. Plan to get there fifteen minutes early and catch up on a little reading while you wait. Some people suggest you set your clocks ahead ten minutes and act as if they showed the real time. I've found this only works for people whose problems are rooted in technical errors. If you are late because of a fear of downtime, you'll never trick yourself into being early.

- **Avoid the "Just One More Task" syndrome.** Is what delays you from getting places on time the tendency to shove in just one more thing—"I'll just make this quick phone call before I leave (or, marinate the roast, or write a quick thank-you, or clean up the kitchen")? Stop! If distractions keep you from getting out the door, turn to the section on minimizing interruptions at the end of this chapter. Remember, handling interruptions is a critical skill for containerizing time and keeping to your plans. Learn to say no.

- **Find your motivation.** Generally it takes a powerful external force to motivate a person to confront a chronic lateness problem. For Natalie, it was the fear of a particularly punitive boss, who'd taken to glaring at her whenever she arrived late for a meeting. Fearful of being on the receiving end of that 600-watt look, Natalie was determined not to be late for meetings with that boss anymore. But remember, the true beneficiary of resolving this issue will be you. The truth is, *you* probably hate being late, hate putting yourself in a vulnerable position by rushing around, hate feeling like you're missing out on things like the appetizers at a friend's dinner party, the beginning of a movie, or a business orientation. Focus on giving yourself permission to relax and enjoy your life a little more.

- **Have something great to do while you wait.** Fill any time you spend waiting with a highly absorbing, totally engaging task. Plan to get places early so that you can call a friend, catch up on a novel, do some paperwork, review your to-do list, or listen to music. People watch and keep a journal. You don't have to stop being busy. You can still keep a packed schedule if that's how you're most comfortable.

- **Understand why lateness upsets others.** The people whom you leave waiting may be polite about it or openly angry with you at times. Step outside your own angst for a minute and understand what it's like to stand in their shoes. Everyone is very, very busy these days. If people have deemed you important enough to have a meeting with, or to get together with, it probably was not easy for them to find that time. They probably also have something very important to do after their get-together with you, tied to another one of *their* big-picture goals. Like you, everyone is trying to balance the various departments of his or her life. When you show up late, people may be disappointed, hurt, or angry that they will have to cut their visit with you short, or have to push something else back to compensate for your lateness. They have also likely broken their necks to get there on time, to be respectful, and to get the most out of their time with you. It's no longer fashionable to be late.

MINIMIZING INTERRUPTIONS

It's tempting to react to interruptions instantly, especially when the people who interrupt are presenting themselves in a desperate, emotional state. But if you stop to handle every interruption the minute it comes up, you'll be pulled in many different directions, become confused and overwhelmed, and end up neglecting your own plans. You can learn to minimize interruptions, whether they are external (caused by other people) or internal (your own need to switch gears).

Can It Wait?

It's important to realize that most crises really aren't crises. When people come to you with so-called urgent demands, the very first thing to do is to consider what is at stake if you don't respond immediately. Think about it. When your coworker rushes into your office with an idea, or when your client e-mails you at 1 a.m. with a question, or when your kid interrupts you while you're on the phone, oftentimes it's because they were struck with a thought and decided to immediately act on it. But it's not urgent. And it doesn't mean you need to drop whatever you're doing. Only 20 percent of interruptions (on the phone, in person, or over e-mail) are true emergencies. The rest can be delayed (within reason and with respect) to a time that works for you.

Try not to schedule yourself so tightly that you have no room to handle any interruptions at all. Crises undoubtedly will arise. The amount of time you should leave open will vary depending on what you do. Look honestly at the demands of your job and your life, and set up systems to allow for the interruptions you generally face.

If you have young children at home, for example, it's unrealistic to think you can plan more than an hour or two of uninterrupted tasks into your day (while they're napping!). Rather than frustrate yourself, accept reality and schedule one to two hours worth of to-dos for each day.

Similarly, if your job requires you to handle a huge volume of phone calls, you may need to allow six hours of unplanned time each day to take care of them. If you work an eight-hour day, that leaves two hours for concentrated work. That may not sound like much, but two uninterrupted hours are probably far more productive than the same amount of time spread out over the day, broken up by phone calls.

You Can Reduce Interruptions

Here are some ways to minimize the most common external interruptions encountered at work and at home.

- **Let people know when you will be unavailable.** If you are about to start something that requires focus, whether it is writing out thank-you notes, taking a long, restorative bath, or writing a report, let the people you live or work with know. Find out if there's anything they need before you "disappear," and let them know when you'll be done.
- **Hire child care, even if you are home.** There's nothing wrong with getting a mother's helper to watch your kids while you are home. That will give you a chance to catch up on tasks you can't do if you are interrupted every five seconds. A couple of hours of relief a few days a week can go a long way.
- **Let voice mail take calls when you are busy.** Just because the phone rings doesn't mean you have to answer it. That includes not picking up the phone as you are headed out the door. Fight your curiosity, stick with whatever you're doing, and let the person leave a message. Let someone else take your calls or have your voice mail take a message. I'm not suggesting you simply ignore callers all together. You have to call people back when you promise you will. The good news is that we tend to be more efficient when we return calls—the average incoming phone call takes eleven minutes, whereas the average outgoing call takes only seven. That's because you've had time to gather your thoughts.

- **Schedule time to read and respond to e-mail.** When you think about it, e-mail is a whole box full of interruptions, requests, and demands from other people. Fight the knee-jerk impulse to check every five minutes, and instead concentrate on your own agenda. When you do check e-mail—and you should at several set times each day—process it fully and clear it out.

- **Choose your quiet hours wisely.** Don't fool yourself into thinking you'll be able to avoid interruptions the minute the kids get home from school or at the end of your workday when everyone is scrambling to tie up loose ends. Find logical times, early in the morning, late at night, while everyone is at lunch, to do your most highly concentrated work.

- **Avoid eye contact.** Whether at work, on a plane, or standing in line at the bank, if you are absorbed in what you are reading (or listening to on your headset), avoid making eye contact with people around you. If you're in an open cubicle at work, turn your desk or your chair away from trafficked areas to avoid making eye contact with every passerby. If that's not possible, place some plants on the periphery of your desk as a boundary. People are less likely to interrupt when they can't make eye contact first.

- **Turn off your instant message function.** If you are bombarded with instant messages from friends and coworkers when you go online to check e-mail, turn off the function. Alternatively, log on with a different account when doing research so no one knows you're there. And be respectful of others' time, too; don't assume that if someone's online he or she has time for a conversation with you. Similarly, install a pop-up blocker to avoid intrusive ads.

- **Schedule regular meeting times for communication.** If you work closely with someone, or need to check in with your spouse and kids regularly, a planned short meeting once or twice a day can be one of the best time-savers in the world—no more having to interrupt one another every ten minutes to exchange information. At home or at the office, you might also plan regular "update" meetings, in person or on the phone.

- **Use e-mail updates.** The nice thing about e-mail communication is that it's accessible twenty-four hours a day. You can communicate a lot of information that others can check when it is convenient for them, and there is no need for a phone call, which can take longer and needs to be coordinated. Alternatively, if you work on projects with other people, keep an electronic project status document in a location that every team member can access. That way anyone can check on the status of the project without interrupting others.

I HAVE SEEN THE ENEMY AND IT'S ME

Of course, it isn't always someone else who interrupts you. Sometimes we interrupt ourselves, and this can be just as counterproductive. Here are some suggestions for minimizing these internal interruptions.

- **Prepare snacks ahead of time and eat before you start.** Rather than going without food for long stretches, or running to the vending machine for a candy bar to tide you over, invest a few minutes in preparing some snacks before you start a long project. Bring a bottle of water to your desk, or keep a thermos bottle of coffee in your office.
- **Keep your planner accessible at all times for jotting down thoughts that come to mind.** When you don't have a single, consistent place to record the new to-dos that you think of or ideas you want to follow up on, it's really tempting to jump up and do them right away. If you create a safe, reliable place to

record this information, you can fight this temptation. Keep your planner nearby and record ideas as they occur to you. At work, everyone should bring their planners to meetings so that they can record new notes to themselves.

- **Keep a notebook or tape recorder on hand to record more complex ideas.** Creative people often need more space for recording their sudden inspirations than a planner can provide, or they need a different medium. If that description fits you, make a habit of carrying a tape recorder or notebook at all times for capturing these brainstorms.
- **Plan for a seventh-inning stretch.** You will need to get up every so often and stretch, unless you want to grow into the shape of your chair. Plan to take a ten-minute break every hour to stretch, or do whatever feels right for you, and then get back to work.

Congratulations. Now you've built a schedule from the inside out, and have the skills you need to safeguard the time you need for accomplishing the tasks most important to you. There's one more step, though . . . Equalize, or learning how to adjust to the only thing we can really count on—that things will inevitably change.

15

EQUALIZE

Time management is not a stagnant process. It is a constant interaction between you, your goals, and the ever-changing rhythms and tempos of life. Life is full of surprises, and the ride can be fun if you have a plan that lets you go with the flow when you need to.

That's what equalizing is: monitoring your situation and then making adjustments that keep you on track. When it comes to time management, you need to equalize daily, bimonthly, and whenever your schedule gets thrown offtrack. Keeping your balance even when your life takes an unexpected turn is an art but one you can learn. This chapter will show you how.

DAILY MONITORING

In order to stay on track (or determine how far offtrack you are), you need to review your planner at least twice each day, once in the morning and again at the end of the day. In addition, you will need to keep your eye on it throughout the day if your schedule is especially busy or contains a wide variety of activities.

At the end of each day, equalize your schedule by doing an evening cleanup of your Time Map. Review your to-do list, and check off everything you got done. Examine the tasks you didn't get to, and think about whether you can delete any of them. A task that was critical in the morning may be irrelevant by the evening. For example, you might have intended to write an important proposal to win over a potential client, but in the meantime your prospect called and placed an order, so now you can cross that task off your list. Tasks you still want to do should be moved forward in your planner. Look over the next few days in your schedule and decide when you will get to them, then record them on the designated day.

I often like to put an open circle "O" to the left of any items I didn't get to, just to give myself a visual picture of the ratio of items "done" versus those "not done" on a given day. This keeps me honest about my time management and helps me to improve; I am constantly refining my own skills of estimating how long things take, delegating, and planning realistically.

BIMONTHLY TUNE-UPS AND OTHER ADJUSTMENTS

Because life moves so rapidly and changes so quickly, you should plan a tune-up on a bimonthly basis. Your Time Map ought to reflect your current goals, priorities, and interests. Every two months, review your Time Map to make sure it supports your current goals. You may need to expand the time allotted for one activity and shrink the time allotted for another.

Though your big-picture goals will rarely change, the activities you choose to support these goals will change over time. Every two months, review your activities and see whether they still warrant a place in your schedule. You may have achieved some of your specific objectives or your priorities may have shifted.

Also, keep in mind that whenever you go through a major life change, you'll have to revamp your Time Map. When you have a baby, you will have to accommodate your little one into your schedule, while still leaving time for yourself and for your relationship with your partner. A new job will require an adjustment; perhaps you will have more interruptions from clients or more meetings to attend than before. If you marry, go back to school, or discover a new interest that you really want to pursue, you will need to fit new activities into your Time Map, adjust the time allotted for other activities, and maybe move a few things around.

HOW TO EQUALIZE DURING TIMES OF CRISIS

There are times in everyone's life when several crises hit you at once and multiple priorities converge. No matter how organized and balanced you have become, occasionally you will find yourself in a situation where everything is urgent, time sensitive, and deadline driven. In these situations, you need to change your attack. Faced with such an onslaught, your impulse may be to jump into reaction mode, answering whatever screams loudest at any given moment. However, this is not the best approach.

The first thing you need to do is to step back from the chaos. You need to gather your thoughts and analyze the situation. This is best done with a little distance. If it's at all possible, put some physical distance between yourself and the situation. Take a walk, a drive, or a shower, or go to the gym. A regrouping moment will enable you to rise above the panic and help you start to make good decisions. Your goal is to come up with a plan of action that spells out exactly what to do and when to do it so that you get to everything important.

APPLY THE SPACE FORMULA

Sort all the tasks that are confronting you. Purge whatever you can. Ask yourself which tasks you can delete or shortcuts you can create.

Also, consider whether you can delegate any of these tasks or any portions of the tasks. When life is this hectic, you need to keep your sanity and energy for the things that matter most. Assign a home on your Time Map only to the most critical activities.

You will have to forgo certain routine activities for a while. You may not be able to cook healthy dinners or get the car washed during this time. Accept that, and don't feel guilty about it.

Even if you are the type of person who thrives on flexibility, when everything is urgent you will have to structure your time tightly. Schedule appointments with yourself for every task on your to-do list. This will keep you focused and productive, and will prevent any one task from monopolizing your time—something you cannot afford when there is so much pressure on you.

Your plan will also allow you to concentrate on just the moment you are in. When you map out where and how you will spend your time, giving each activity a place in your schedule, you no longer have to worry about how you will fit everything in. You've already decided that, and you are free to focus on the task at hand.

No matter how intense things get, make sure that you always preserve some time for self-renewal. Decide which activity most effectively recharges you (going to the gym, getting a massage, making love) and make time for it. It will give you the strength you need to get through the crisis. Take care of yourself: Eat well, get enough rest and exercise. Select one regular activity from each of the other critical departments of your life (reading to your kids, taking a walk with your mate, speaking with your friends) and fit that in. Then let everything else go and focus on the crisis.

Get back to your ideal balance as soon as you can. When the crisis is over, you may need to spend a few weeks compensating for the things you were unable to get to during that time. Be aware, however, that sometimes crises like these require a permanent adjustment of your Time Map because your circumstances have changed for good—and hopefully for the good. After each crisis, evaluate your Time Map to see if it needs to be adjusted.

FORGIVE YOURSELF FOR YOUR FAILURES

If you don't get to everything you wanted to get to in any given day or during a crisis, don't beat yourself up. Very few people ever finish every last thing on their to-do lists. As long as you are regularly getting to all the important things in your life, you don't have to worry that you haven't gotten to every single item.

Because life changes so frequently, your priorities may change with it. Your moods are not static, and your energy levels will fluctuate. A project you thought would be almost effortless turns out to be very difficult and draining, which will in turn influence how you function for the rest of the week. There are circumstances that may distract you: relationship problems or illnesses. There are also circumstances that energize you: You might fall in love and suddenly have enough energy and confidence to tackle two days' worth of tasks in one morning. Give yourself room to ride those waves, and always keep your eye on your planner so that you can make adjustments.

The worst thing to do is berate yourself for not getting everything done, for periodically procrastinating, or for slowing down from time to time. The time and energy you spend feeling guilty can extend a less-than-productive morning into a less-than-productive day. Even the most energetic and efficient people occasionally have off days. The thing that makes them good time managers is that they realize these are a part of life. They forgive themselves, make the necessary adjustments to their schedules, and move on.

If you have an off day, take a few moments to analyze what went wrong. Were you overbooked, underbooked, too tired, or especially stressed? Was there an event that caused you to abandon your plans? Can you avoid this problem in the future?

The most liberating aspect of time management from the inside out is that it is a way of creating a life that nurtures you and makes you feel good. You are the master of your own life, and while you can't control all the events around you, you can control your reactions to those events. Instead of dwelling on what you haven't achieved, give yourself credit for what you have been able to do.

CELEBRATE YOUR SUCCESSES

Specific moments of achievement give us an opportunity to celebrate. So often we tend to gloss over those moments in our rush to move on to the next thing on the to-do list. When we do that, we cheat ourselves of one of the great pleasures in life.

Take time to celebrate your victories. Finally land a big contract you've worked your butt off to get? Enjoy the moment of triumph—whoop it up! Call a friend, break out the bubbly, buy yourself some theater tickets—do something fun and exhilarating. When you have goals and you're achieving them, luxuriate in that wonderful sense of accomplishment! Relish this feeling, and invite the people in your life to relish it with you. This will bolster your self-esteem, and it will invigorate you to go on achieving and enjoying.

When you implement the techniques in this book, at first it will feel like work. At some point, though, you will notice that your time is under control and you are working toward goals that are meaningful to you—and achieving them. You will pick up momentum and will begin to feel full of confidence and in love with your life. This is the true meaning of success, and you should celebrate it!

Appendix A

Time Map Worksheet

Appendix A—Time Map

Time	Monday	Tuesday	Wednesday	Thursday	Friday	Saturday	Sunday
	Wake up	Wake up	Wake up	Wake up	Wake up	Wake up	Wake up
	Sleep	Sleep	Sleep	Sleep	Sleep	Sleep	Sleep

Appendix B

Sources for Time Management and Organizing Products

PRODUCTS

Time-Management Tools

Act!: www.act.com, (877) 501-4496
At-A-Glance: www.meadwestvaco.com, (888) 205-3324
Day Runner: www.dayrunner.com, (800) 365-9327
Day-Timer: www.daytimer.com, (800) 457-5702
Franklin Covey: www.franklincovey.com, (800) 819-1812
Filofax: www.filofaxusa.com, (877) 234-2426, x0
Harold Taylor: www.taylorintime.com, (800) 361-8463
TimeDesign: www.timedesign.com, (800) 501-4496

PDAs, Palmtops, HPCs

Casio: www.casio.com, (800) 836-8580
Hewlett-Packard: www.hp.com, (800) 752-0900
Palm: www.palm.com, (800) 881-7256
Psion: www.psion.com
Sharp: www.sharp-usa.com, (800) BE-SHARP
Toshiba: www.toshiba.com, (800) GO-TOSHIBA

Online Calendars, Schedulers, PIMs

These sites keep your personal or group calendar, scheduling, and contact information online.

Yahoo! Calendar: www.calendar.yahoo.com
Visto: www.visto.com, (866) 828-4786

Online Software Resources

Read reviews or see screenshots and download trial versions of PIMs and other helpful time-saving software.

SoftSeek: www.softseek.com
ZD Net: www.zdnet.com

CATALOGS AND STORES

Home

Bed, Bath and Beyond: www.bedbathandbeyond.com, (800) GO-BEYOND
Container Store: www.containerstore.com, (888) 266-8246
Exposures: www.exposuresonline.com, (888) 263-9850
Frontgate: www.frontgate.com, (888) 263-9850
Hold Everything: www.holdeverything.com, (800) 421-2264
Ikea: www.ikea.com, (800) 434-4532
Levenger: www.levenger.com, (800) 667-8034
Lillian Vernon: www.lillianvernon.com, (800) 901-9291
Pottery Barn: www.potterybarn.com, (888) 779-5176

Office/Home Office

Bindertek: www.bindertek.com, (800) 456-3453
Ikea: www.ikea.com, (800) 434-4532

Levenger: www.levenger.com, (800) 434-4532

Mobile Office Outfitters: www.mobilegear.com, (616) 971-0080

Office Depot: www.officedepot.com, (800) 463-3768

Office Max: www.officemax.com, (800) 283-7674

Quill: www.quillcorp.com, (800) 982-3400

Reliable: www.reliable.com, (800) 359-5000

Staples: www.staples.com, (800) 378-2753

ADDITIONAL RESOURCES

Public Storage Self-Storage (pickup and delivery): www.publicstorage.com, (866) 44-MOVING

The National Association of Professional Organizers—information and referral hotline (for professional organizers in your area): www.napo.net, (847) 375-4746

Julie Morgenstern's Task Masters: www.juliemorgenstern.com, 1-86-ORGANISE

Appendix C

Suggested Further Reading

TIME

Breathing Space, Jeff Davidson. MasterMedia, Ltd., 1991.

First Things First, Stephen R. Covey, A. Roger Merrill, and Rebecca R. Merrill. Simon & Schuster, 1994.

How to Take Control of Your Time and Life, Alan Lakein. Peter H. Wyden, Inc., 1973.

It's About Time! The Six Styles of Procrastination and How to Overcome Them, Linda Sapadin and Jack Maguire. Viking, 1996.

Making Time Work for You, Harold L. Taylor. Harold Taylor Time Consultants, 1998.

The Power of Full Engagement, Jim Loehr and Tony Schwartz. Free Press, 2003.

The Power of Habit, Jack D. Hodge. 1st Books Library, 2003.

The Procrastinator's Handbook, Rita Emmett. Walker & Co., 2000.

Take Time for Your Life, Cheryl Richardson. Broadway Books, 1998.

Ten Days to Faster Reading, Abby Marks-Beale. Warner Books, 2001.

Time Management for Unmanageable People, Ann McGee-Cooper and Duane Trammell. Bantam Books, 1994.

Time Management for the Creative Person, Lee Silber. Three Rivers Press, 1998.

GOAL-SETTING/INSPIRATION

Change Your Thinking, Change Your Life, Brian Tracy. John Wiley & Sons, 2003.

Finding Your Own North Star, Martha Beck. Three Rivers Press, 2002.

Goals: How to Get Everything You Want—Faster Than You Ever Thought Possible, Brian Tracy. Berrett-Koehler Publisher, 2003.

I Could Do Anything, If Only I Knew What It Was, Barbara Sher. Delacorte Press, 1994.

Live the Life You Love, Barbara Sher. Dell Publishing, 1996.

Now, Discover Your Strengths, Marcus Buckingham and Donald Clifton. Free Press, 2001.

Optimal Thinking: How to Be Your Best Self, Rosalene Glickman. John Wiley & Sons, 2002.

Take Yourself to the Top, Laura Berman. Fortgang, 1998.

You Can Make It Happen, Stedman Graham. Free Press, 1998.

ACKNOWLEDGMENTS

I am so grateful to the following people for their significant contributions:

To Lisa Considine, my amazing editor, for becoming a true champion for this book, and a genuine partner in making it happen.

To Daniel Reid, for so attentively coordinating the technical elements of every page and illustration.

To Cloe Axelson, for helping me shape this material for the platform, and then convert those discoveries to this book.

To Carol Crespo, for your tremendous work on the first edition, which provided so much of the foundation for this second edition.

To Joni Evans, my agent, for your limitless and generous support.

To John Sterling, publisher, Jennifer Barth, editor in chief, Maggie Richards, sales and marketing director, Elizabeth Shreve, publicity director, Kenn Russell, managing editor, and Tom Nau, production chief, at Henry Holt, for making this second edition possible in record time.

To David Sobel, editor of the first edition, and Faith Hamlin, my original agent for this book.

To my clients, audiences, and readers, for sharing your feedback, stories, challenges, and successes over the years.

To Ellen Kosloff, Anna Hick, and Diana Petrushevskaya, of Task Masters, for managing the office around my writing schedule.

To my family and friends, for always being there.

And to Jessi . . . you are the true queen of time management!

INDEX

ABC News' "The Note," 90
Act! (software), 116
activities. *See also* tasks; Time Map
  adding one you're not getting done, to
    Time Map, 187–89
  bimonthly tune-ups, 258
  core, Time Map and, 175
  cutting, 151
  chart of goals and, 162, 169–70
  choosing, to furthur goals, 166–69
  creating Time Map to fit, 189–90
  defined, vs. goals, 158–59
  defined, vs. tasks, 199–200
  defining goals and, 157–72
  layering, 190–91
  more than one category and, 151
  not making time for, and goal clarity,
    152–53
  paring down, 168–69
  revising annually, 169–72
  Time Map and structuring of, 174
add it up step, 62, 64
addresses
  labels, 73
  paper planner and, 115
analyze, 3, 103–53
  applying results, 132–33
  closet metaphor, and weeks as
    containers, 145–52
  energy and rhythms and, 136–39
  life categories and, 141–44
  personal balance checkup and, 141–53

  time-management preferences and,
    133–36
  variety and, 138–39
  what's not working and, 129–32
  what's working and, 126–29
annual events, 122–24
anxiety, waiting for others and, 249–51
appointments
  boundaries of, 135
  crisis and, 260
  cushion of time before, 250
  to-do's as, 238–39
  wall or desk calendar and, 108
articles and clippings, 88
assign step, 200, 201, 227–39
  arranging day and, 233–37
  creating start and stop times and,
    229–31
  funneling tasks, into Time Map and,
    236–37
  honoring decisions and, 238–39
  maintaining balance with trade-offs,
    237
  natural rhythms and, 234–36
  proactive, vs. reactive, 228–29
  sandbox and, 232–33
assistant's to-do list, 113
At-a-Glance, 110
attack, 3, 6, 199–262
  SPACE Formula and, 199–201
  assign, 227–39
  containerize, 241–56

attack (*cont'd*)
  equalize, 257–62
  purge, 211–26
  sort, 200–210
avoidance, 248

baby announcements and gifts, 87–88
backlog of paper, 82–85. *See also* paper
    clutter
  getting real, 84
  quick sort and, 82–83
balance, 3–4, 36
  assigning home and, 228–29, 237
  before and after Time Map and,
    181–86
  checkup, 141–53
  common stuck points, 150–52
  defining goals and, 159–60
  deleting tasks to keep, 211–12
  evaluating time log, 151–52
  goal clarity and, 152–53
  importance of, 188
  instant fix, with Time Map, 187–89
  maintaining, with trade-offs, 237
  reexamining, 153
  restoring, after crisis, 260–61
  simplify categories, 141–44
  Time Map and, 174
  tracking time and, 143–52
Balance Tracker, 192, 201
Beck, Martha, 163
beginner, delegating to, 221
big-picture goals, 2, 30, 157–72
  activities vs., 158–59
  assigning a home and, 235, 238
  defining, 157–72
  chart, 162, 169–70
  choosing activities for, 166–69
  clarity of, 171–72
  clarity of, balance as indicator and,
    152–53
  clarity of vision and, 161
  connecting daily to-dos to, 205–6
  containerizing and, 241
  crystal ball exercise, 165–66
  daily tasks and, 199

deciding what tasks to delete and,
    211–12
  defined, vs. activities, 158–59
  dreaming and, 159–60
  difficulty articulating, 163–66
  eliminating tasks that don't serve, 20
  focusing on, to conquer
    procrastination, 243
  help with articulating, 163–66
  honoring decisions and, 238–39
  how long tasks take and, 208
  how to define, 159–60
  joy journal, 165
  life categories and, 141–44, 159–60
  releasing ones you don't want, 164–65
  revising activities list and, 169–72
  SPACE formula and, 201
  sorting tasks according to, 202–6
  Time Map and, 176–80, 189–90,
    196
  unclear, 27–29
  unsure how to pursue, 169
  writing down, 160–62
big-picture view, 13–14, 157
bill paying
  center for, 71–72
  estimating time required for, 44–45
  no place in schedule for, 146
  sandbox for, 232
  shortcuts, 71
bimonthly tune-ups, 258–59
birthdays, 72, 115, 122
boss
  delegating to, 77
  disorganized, 26–27
  priorities and, 238–39
  saying no to, 214
boundaries, setting, 55, 135–36
briefcase, clutter in, 81, 97
brochures, 87, 88
business cards, 87

calendar
  company computer network, 116–17
  wall or desk, 106, 108–9
Canfield, Jack, 161

CardScan software, 87
caretaker, 32–34
car maintenance, 122
catalogs, 88, 97
catchphrase, adopting, 245
categories. *See* life categories
Center for Democracy and Technology, 96
change, fear of, 31–32
chaos, stepping back from, 259. *See also* conquistator of chaos; crises
Checkbox Time Card, 192–93
checkups, 122
Chicken Soup for the Soul (Canfield and Hansen), 161
children
  child care for, 253
  interruptions and, 252
  staying home with sick, 205
cleanup time, 50, 235
client, saying no to, 214
clipping services, 90
clock, setting ahead, 250
closet metaphor
  before and after Time Maps and, 181–86
  life categories and, 142
  schedule and, 38–40
  SPACE forumla and, 200–201
  weeks as containers and tracking time and, 144–52
clothes
  laying out night before, 70
  master travel checklist, 72
  repair center and, 71
  simplifying, 72, 162
clutter, household, 69. *See also* paper clutter
  daily pickup, 163
  eliminating, 164
cluttered schedule, 38–40
color
  of clothes, 162
  coding files, 94–95, 165
common goal, disorganized partner and, 26–27

community, 142
commuting time, 150
completion, fear of, 34
computer planners, 106, 107, 116–17. *See also* personal digital assistants (PDAs)
  annual events and, 122
  format and features, 120–21
  marrying, with paper, 117–20
  paper vs., 131–32
  portability and, 116
  synchronizing, with PDA, 117
  visual/tactile people and, 121–22
concentration, 19–20, 149
  developing tolerance for, 52
  times of crisis and, 260
  reducing interruptions and, 254
conferences, 87
conquistador of chaos, 29–30, 243, 246
Consumer Protection Association, 97
contact manager, 116
Contact (software), 116
Containerize step, 34, 35, 200, 201, 241–56
  chronic lateness and, 245–51
  minimizing external interruptions and, 251–55
  minimizing internal interruptions and, 255–56
  procrastination and, 242–45
  weeks as containers and, 145–52
cooking, 69
coupons, 88, 89
coworker, delegating to, 76–77
creativity, 34–36, 191–92
creator, editor vs., 34
credit card, 71
crises
  conquistador of crisis and, 29–30
  equalizing schedule during, 259–62
  leaving time for, 26, 252
  seeing if it can wait, 252–53
  Sudden Opportunity List and, 193–94
crystal ball exercise, 165–66

daily
    monitoring, 257–58
    time to process paper, 96–99
day, arranging, 233–37
    natural rhythms and, 234–36
    Time Map and, 236–37
Day Runner, 110
Day-Timer, 110, 111
deadlines
    preferences and, 134
    self-imposed, 134, 244–45
decision making
    decide step and, 62, 64–66
    filtering tools for, 201
    how long task will take and, 208–10
    keep or toss, ten questions, 89
    procrastination and, 243
    Time Map and, 175
delay task, 64
    defined, 65
    paper clutter and, 85
    purge step and, 225–26
delegating, 20–21, 64, 66, 85, 219–25
    caretaker and, 33
    crises and, 260
    defined, 66
    depending on others and, 220
    exercise, 75–76
    fear of becoming dispensable and,
        220–21
    finding best person and, 221–22
    guilt and, 220
    hiring others and, 222–23
    household chores and, 132–33
    keeping options open and, 222–25
    paper clutter and, 85
    psychological factors and, 219–20
    purge step and, 219–25
    three steps of, 79
    time required for, 79–80
    too busy for, 220
    what to delegate, 75–76
    who to delegate to, 76–78
    writing instructions and, 132–33
delete task, 211–16
    crisis and, 259

daily monitoring and, 258
defined, 64–65
finding tasks to cut, when tracking
    time, 151
paper clutter and, 85–89
departments. See life categories
depression, 24–25
different step, 243
digital planners. see electronic planners
diminish task, 64
    defined, 65–66
    paper clutter and, 85
    purge step and, 216–19
directions, 115
Direct Marketing Association Mail
    Preference Service, 96
disorganized
    partner, 26
    physical environment, 22
distractions. See interruptions
doctors, 24–25
downtime, 31–32, 246
drafts, 88
duplicate printouts, 88
duration, assigning tasks by, 235

editor, creator vs., 34
electronic device, time required to hook
    up, 45–46
electronic planners (digital), 106,
    117–20. See also computer
    planners; personal digital assistants
    advanced features, 117
    brands, 117
    customizing, 122–24
    linear/digital people and, 107–8
    marrying paper and, 117–20
    month-view printout, 118–19
    pros and cons of, 121
    portability of, 117
    to-do list and, 64
    visual/tactile people and, 121–22
electronic project status document, 255
e-mail, 81, 231, 254, 255
energy cycles
    assigning tasks and, 236

identifying, 136–37
  health problems and, 24–25
  procrastination and, 202
  setting aside wrong time and, 19–20
  sources and rhythms and, 136–38
  Time Map and, 190
  variety and, 138–39, 235
equal, delegating to, 221
equalize step, 200, 201, 257–62
  bimonthly tune-ups and, 258–59
  celebrating successes and, 262
  daily monitoring and, 257–58
  failures and, 261–62
  times of crisis and, 259–61
errands, 69–71
execute your plan step, 62, 66–80
  in action, 67–68
  delegating and, 75–80
  how to do anything faster and, 68–75
exercise, 152
expense tracking, 74, 113, 115
expert, delegating to, 174, 221
external realities, 18, 24–27
  health limits energy, 24–25
  interruption-rich environment, 26
  other people's chaos, 26–27
  transition period and, 25
eye contact, 254

failures
  fear of, 30–31
  forgiving yourself for, 261–62
family, 142
  big-picture goals and, 159
  delegating to, 77, 223–25
  scheduling meeting times, 254–55
Family Night, 147
fear
  of articulating goals, 163–64
  of criticism, 34–35
  of completion, 34, 243
  of disrupting status quo, 31
  of downtime, 31–32, 246, 248–49, 250
  of failure or success, 30–31, 243
  of finding out where you spend your
    time, 145

of losing creativity, 35–36
  of structure, 191
filing
  as boring, 94
  color coding and, 94
  estimating time required for, 45
  everything, and tracking with planner,
    85–86
  folders, 89, 94–95
  improving system, 93–96
  labeling and, 95
  location of workstation and, 93
  location of mail station and, 96
  straight-line, 95
  tab coding and, 95
  too complicated, 93–94
  topics and, 93–94
Filofax, 110
finances, 77, 142
  big-picture goals and, 159
first draft, 74
five-minute "sudden opportunities,"
  194
foundation, 2
four Ds, 211–26
  delay, 64, 65, 85, 225–26
  delegate, 64, 66, 85, 219–25
  delete, 64–65, 85–89, 211–16,
    258–59
  diminish, 64–66, 85, 216–19
Franklin Covey Planner, 110
friend
  delegating to, 77
  goal clarity and, 152–53
friendship, 142, 159

geography, assigning tasks by, 236
getting out door faster, 70–71
"getting real" boxes
  caretaker, 33
  chronic lateness, 247–49
  defining goals, and office location,
    28–29
  delegating household chores, 78,
    132–33
  estimating time for household task, 49

"getting real" boxes (cont'd)
  estimating time for writing client
    reports, 42–43
  finding right planner, 104–5
  getting kids out in morning,
    55–56
  hidden pockets of time, 146–47
  inbox, 98
  multitasking prevents proper
    calculating, 52
  paper clutter and mortgage
    application, 86
  paper piles at home, 84
  perfectionism and shortcuts, 218–
    19
  Post-it planner, 108–9
  saying no, as volunteer, 214–16
  Sunday paper, 92
  Time Map and derailing, 179
  WADE Formula in action, 67–68
  what's working, 129
  working with clients vs. alone,
    135–36
  writing sandbox, 232–33
gifts, 72, 87–88, 115
goals. See big-picture goals; common
    goal
Goldmine (software), 116
greeting cards, 72, 89
groceries, 69
grounding activities, 25
guilt, downtime and, 31–32

Hansen, Mark Victor, 161
have-tos, converting, to want-tos,
    203–5
health, 142
  goals, Time Map and, 189–90
  problems, 24–25
hidden pockets of time, 145–48, 151
hidden time costs, 50
holidays, 72. See also greeting cards
home. See also family
  big-picture goals and, 159
  category, 142
  weekend to-do list, 229

household chores. See also specific chores
  cleaning, 69–70
  delegating, 223–25
  Family Night and, 147
  how to delegate, 78
  no place in schedule for, 146
  tracking time and, 150–52

imbalances, frequent shifts and,
    149–50. See also balance
in-box, 98
individuality, 126
instant messages, 254
instincts, trusting, 243
instructions, 89
interest level, assigning tasks by, 236
interruptions, 26
  chronic lateness and, 246, 250
  external, 201, 253–54
  internal, 201, 255–56
  minimizing, 241, 251–55
  reducing, 253–55
  time, estimating, 51, 252–53
invitations, 89, 213

joy
  giving self permission to achieve, 163
  journal, 165
junk mail, 88
"just one more task" syndrome, 250

keep or toss questions, 89
kitchen countertop, 81
knowledge, 142, 159

last-minute reminder list, 73
lateness, chronic, 4, 241, 245–51
  motivation for curing, 250–51
  pinpointing problem, 246–49
  respecting anxiety and, 249–51
  understanding why others are upset
    by, 251
laundry
  have-to or want-to, 204–5
  speed up, 70
letters, 45, 73–74

life
    circumstances of, goals and activities
        and, 69
    designing, through time
        management, 12–13
    giving focus to, by defining goals,
        159–60
    major changes in, revamping Time
        Map after, 258–59
    management, time management as, 57
life categories (departments)
    activities under more than one, 151
    common stuck points, 150–152
    crystal ball exercise and, 166
    goals and activities and, 167–68
    neglected, 151
    overloading, 207
    paring down activities and, 168–69
    setting big-picture goals for each,
        159–62, 166
    simplifying, 141–44
    snapshot of, by tracking time spent
        on, 148–52
    snapshot of what you want to
        accomplish and, 169, 170
    sorting tasks by, 203, 207
    struggling to keep distinct, 152
    Time Map and, 174
linear/digital people, 107–8
linear/digital planners, 110–13. See also
        electronic planners; personal
        digital assistant
    pros and cons, 114
    visual/tactile people and, 121–22

magazines, 88, 90
Magic of Thinking Big, The (Schwarz), 62
mail, 81–82
    being decisive about, 97
    daily time to process, 96
    getting off mailing lists, 96–97
    no place in schedule for, 146
    sorting, 203
    station, 96
maintenance, time required for, 6. See
        also equalize step

"making time tangible" concept, 37–57.
        See also closet metaphor
    cluttered closet metaphor and, 38–40
    defined, 37–38
    "how long will it take" and, 40–41
    why we don't ask how long it will
        take, 42–46
management consultant, 28–29
Marks-Beale, Abby, 91, 92
meeting
    memos, 86
    notes, 87
    scheduling regular family, 254–55
miscalculating how long tasks take, 20,
        40, 42, 44–46
miserable task
    combining, with enjoyable task, 244
    Misery Task Basket for, 98
monthly-view format, 110, 118–19
mortgage application, 86
mothers. See also children; family;
        working parents
    getting kids off to school, 55–56
    interruptions and, 26
    Post-it planner for, 108–9
    Time Map for, 184–86
motivation, 9–40
    big-picture view and, 13–14
    containerizing and, 241
    discovering, 9–12
    finding, to cure lateness, 250–51
    goals vs. activities and, 158–59
    time management and, 132–33
    writing compelling reason and, 12
multitasking, 51, 52, 88, 89
    layering activities and, 90–91

natural rhythms, 134. See also energy
        cycles
    arranging day and, 234–36
    exercises, 137–38
newspapers, 88
    Sunday, 92
no, learning to say, 32–34, 43, 212–16
    practicing, 213–14
notebook, 256

Now Update (software), 116
nutrition, 24–25

obstacles, organizing time vs. space, 6.
    See also psychological factors;
    technical errors
off days, analyzing, 261–62
office. *See also* work
    desk, paper clutter, 81
    organizing, 22
one hour "sudden opportunity," 194
one-page-per-day format, 112
online
    greeting cards, 72
    paying bills, 71
    shopping, 69
opportunities, 161
Oprah Winfrey Show, 67
Organizing from the Inside Out, 5–6, 22,
    94
organizing space, 22
Outlook (software), 116
outside help, 77, 222–23
overwhelming tasks, breaking down,
    244. *See also* projects

pace
    balance and, 152
    personal preferences and, 4
packing and unpacking
    estimating time required for, 45
    making faster, 72–73
    unpacking immediately, 73
PalmPilot, 74, 104, 116–17
    m130, 117
    month-view printout, 118–19
    Treo 600, 117
paper-based planners, 104, 108–16
    brand, 110
    choosing, 115
    close-up view, 110
    electronic vs., 106, 131–32
    corresponding computer software,
        120–21
    customizing and taking ownership of,
        122–24

formats, 110
    marrying electronic and, 117–20
    monthly-view, 110
    one-page-per-day format, 110, 112
    portable, 110–16
    Post-it to-dos in, 123
    pros and cons, 115–16, 121
    to-do list and, 64, 104
paper clutter, 2
    assess backlog step, 82–85
    daily time to process, 96–99
    keep or toss ten questions, 89
    organizing, 22
    quick-start program for, 61, 62,
        81–99
    stay ahead of game step, 90–99
    volume problem, 82
    weed it down step, 82, 85–89
paper shredder, 88
partner, disorganized, 26–27
passive regression, 91
PDAs. *See* personal digital assistants
people-oriented tasks, 135–36
perfectionism, 34–35
    deadlines and, 244
    shortcuts and, 217–18
permission, giving yourself, 163–64
personal digital assistant (PDAs),
    117–20
    format and features, 120–21
    marrying paper with, 117–20
    month-view printout, 118–19
    pros and cons, 117
    synchronizing, with computer, 117
personal information manager (PIMs),
    116–17
personal style, 4, 12–13. *See also* energy
    cycle; natural rhythms;
    psychological factors
    relationship to time and, 125–38
    Time Map as reflection of, 195–96
PIM. *See* personal information manager
planner. *See also* electronic planners;
    paper-based planners; personal
    digital assistant
    assigning a home to tasks and, 227

brands, 106, 120–21
choosing, 21–22, 103–24
electronic options, 116–21
eliminating paper clutter with, 85–86
format, features, and brands, 106, 120–21
keeping accessible, 124, 255–56
linear/digital for visual/tactile people, 121–22
marrying paper and electronic, 117–20
mastering features of, 106
need to refer to, constantly, 124
as only place for to-dos, 227
paper, vs. electronic, 106
paper, visual tactile people and, 107, 108–16
as paper management tool, 86
portable, 110–16
pros and cons table, 115–16
recording everything on, 124
rescheduling unfinished tasks in, 124
reviewing daily, 124
size of, 110
SPACE formula and, 201
spontaneous shopping lists in, 69
stationary, vs. portable, 106, 109
stationary computer, 116–17
stationary, wall or desk, 108–9
studying, to find where you spend time, 145, 148–49
taking ownership of, 122–24
three common mistakes, 103–4
"tracking time for tasks" exercise, 47–52
two-page-per-day format, 110, 113–14
visual/tactile, 106–7
week-on-two pages format, 110–11
"write it down" step and, 63
writing legibly in, 124
planning time, 22–23
pop-up blocker, 254
postcards, 73
Post-it Notes
planner, 108–9
to-dos and, 123

prep time, 235
"present the job" step, 79
priorities and prioritizing
asking other person to, 214, 238
Time Map and, 174, 176–80
to-dos and, 238
procrastination, 4, 39
conquering, 241, 242–46
miscalculating how long tasks take and, 42, 44
overly complex task and, 21
targeting three tasks exercise for, 46–47
productivity, 51, 52, 146
project
breaking down complex, 21, 53, 244
estimating time for big, 53–56
overstuffed file from, 87
paper-planner and, 115
skipping steps on big, 74–75
psychological factors, 18, 27–36
chronic lateness and, 245–46
conquistador of crisis, 29–30
delegating and, 79, 219–20
fear of completion, 34
fear of disrupting status quo, 31
fear of downtime, 31–32
fear of failure or success, 30–31
fear of stifling creativity, 35–36
four Ds and, 211
need for perfection, 34–35
need to be caretaker, 32–34
procrastination and, 242–43
time organization, 6
unclear goals, 27–29
public relations, 26
purge step, 20, 21, 25, 200, 201, 211–26. See also four Ds
delegating tasks, 219–25
deleting tasks, 211–16
puttering, 242

quick-start program, 2, 61–99
how to do anything faster, 68–75
managing daily onslaught, with WADE Formula, 62–68

quick-start program (*cont'd*)
    optimizing resources by delegating,
        76–80
    where paper meets time, 81–99
quiet hours, choosing, 254

reading, 90, 91
real estate business, 26
realistic workload, 20
recipes, 89
recording options, 123
refreshment time, 51, 149
regrouping, 259
remembering what to do, 21–22
"remember to take" checklist, 70–71
Repair Center, 71
research
    as goal, 169
    material, 88
resources, optimizing, 75–80. *See also*
        delegating
"review and evaluate result" step, 79
Richardson, Cheryl, 163
right brain, 35
road maps, 89
romance, 142, 159, 164
room, organizing, 22
routine
    evaluating yours, 152
    forgoing, during crisis, 260
running-list basis, 234

salespeople, 26, 110
sandbox, 232–33
schedule. *See also* planner; Time Map
    cluttered, before and after, 38–40
    creating Time Map to reflect
        priorities and, 189–90
    fitting tasks into, 206–8
    grid to track time and do math,
        149–50
    personal preferences and, 13–14, 134
    setting aside right time and, 19–20
    setting specific time for important
        tasks and, 19
    Time Map as way to structure, 175

what throws off, 151
where does task and to-do belong in,
        206–8
school periods, Time Map and, 174
"select one" rule, 105
self, 142
    -assessment, 125
    big-picture goals and, 159
    time for, in times of crisis, 260
self-doubt exercise, 165–66
service-based industries, 26
service contracts, 89
setup time, 50
seventh-inning stretch, 256
Sher, Barbara, 163
shopping
    lists, paper planners and, 115
    master list, 69
    online, 69
    spontaneous, 70
shortcuts, 216–17, 259
significance, assigning home by, 235
sleep problems, 24–25
snacks, 255
solitary tasks, 135–36
sort step, 135, 199–210
    backlog of to-dos and, 151–53
    big-picture goals and, 202–6
    how long task will take and, 208–10
    where task belongs in schedule,
        206–8
space, disorganized, 22
SPACE formula, 6, 200–202
    assign, 227–39
    containerize, 241–56
    equalize, 257–62
    purge, 211–26
    sort, 199–210
    times of crisis and, 259–61
spare time, 19
spirituality, 142, 159
spontaneity, 234
spouse
    disorganized, 26
    time alone with, 147
staff, delegating to, 76

starting and stopping tasks, 229–31
"stay ahead of game" step, 90–99
  daily time for paperwork and, 96–99
  improve filing system and, 93–96
  reduce reading pile and, 90–92
Steele, Danielle, 161
stewing time, 50
strategize, 5–6
  defining goals and activities and,
    157–72
  designing life you love and, 3
  time mapping and, 173–196
structure
  creativity and, 35–36
  despising, Time Map alternatives
    and, 191–95
  fear of, 35–36
  how much to use, 233–34
  times of crisis and, 260
subscriptions, 88, 90
successes
  celebrating, 262
  fear of, 31
Sudden Opportunity List, 193–94, 201

tape recorder, 256
tasks. See also to-dos
  assigning homes for, 227–39
  conquering lateness and, 250
  containerizing, 241–56
  daily, vs. goals and activities 199–200
  deleting or moving forward
    unfinished, 258
  equalizing, 257–62
  estimating time for, 4, 20, 40–41,
    44–46, 208–10
  estimating time for, improving by
    tracking actual time, 46–52
  finding what can be cut, by tracking
    time, 151
  fitting into cluttered schedule, 38
  fitting into schedule, by category,
    206–8
  have no home error, 19
  "just one more" syndrome, 250
  as object, 40

overly complex, 21
purging, 211–26
sorting, 201–10
SPACE formula and, 200–201
start and stop times for, 229
targeting three, exercise, 46–47
time of day for, 152
teamwork, 66
technical errors, 18, 19–24
  absence of planning time, 22–23
  can't remember what to do, 21–22
  miscalculating time tasks take, 20,
    40, 42
  overly complex tasks, 21
  space disorganized, 22
  tasks have no home, 19
  unrealistic workload, 23–24
  wrong person for job, 20–21
  wrong time set for, 19–20
telephone calls
  e-mail vs., 255
  messages, 87
  scheduling, 231
  setting aside time for, 252–53
  solicitors, saying no to, 213
  voice mail and, 253
telephone numbers, 115
templates, 73, 218
Ten Days to Faster Reading (Marks-
    Beale), 91
thank-you note, 45, 73–74
thirty-minute "sudden opportunity"
    tasks, 194
thyroid problem, 25
time. See also time, estimating; Time
    Map; tracking time
  adding cushion of, 250
  amount required, to organize time vs.
    space, 5–6
  boundaries, 135–36, 186
  common stuck points, 150–52
  finding out where you spend, 141–52
  hidden pockets of, 145–48, 151
  how to do anything faster, 68–75
  intangibility of, 37
  life categories and, 141–44, 168–69

time (cont'd)
  making tangible, 37–57
  need for planning time and, 22–23
  organizing space vs., 5–6, 38–40
  processing paperwork and, 96–99
  setting starting and stopping times, 229
  SPACE formula and, 200–201
  understanding personal relationship to, 125–39
time, estimating, 3, 44–52, 208–10
  actual, vs. estimated, 47–48
  big projects and, 53–56
  deciding how much, to assign to task and, 232–33
  delegating and, 79–80
  as gateway skill to time management, 56–57
  how long other people take and, 54–56
  improving skills, 46–52
  improving skills, to cure lateness, 250
  lateness and, 246
  log, 47
  miscalculating, 20
  target three tasks exercise, 46–47
  to-dos in paper clutter and, 83–84
  tracking in planner exercise, 47–52
Time Design, 110
time limit, 244
time management. See also planner; schedule; SPACE Formula; time, estimating; Time Map; WADE Formula
  analyzing what's working and not working and, 126–32
  applying results of analysis, 132–33
  daily monitoring and, 258
  defining, from inside out, 12–13
  defining goals and activities and, 157–72
  as energizing, 262
  estimating time as gateway skill to good, 56–57
  exercise, 133–34
  personal preferences and, 133–34
  personal style and, 4

  products to aid, 265–67
  tools to get on track and, 14–15
Time Map, 26, 173–96
  assigning tasks to, 236
  adding one activity you're not getting done, 187–89
  adjusting, 196
  alternatives to, if you despise structure, 191–95
  for alternative work/life rhythms, 194–95
  assigning home step, 233–34
  benefits of, 175
  before and after, 181–86
  bimonthly tune-ups, 258–59
  creating, 189–90
  crisis management, 260–61
  customizing, 195–96
  daily monitoring, 257–59
  defined, 173–74
  honoring decisions and, 238–39
  instant balance fix, 187–89
  layering activities and, 190–91
  major life changes and, 258–59
  not for everyone, 175
  as reflection of goals and priorities, 176–80
  as reflection of personal preferences, 195–96
  SPACE Formula and, 201
  vertical, 195
time of day, 152
time of year, 169
to-do list
  assigning homes to, 230
  boundaries and, 135–36
  carrying over, to next day, 108
  daily monitoring, 257
  estimating time required for, 40–41, 44–46, 208–10
  examining, to see what gets done, 149
  grouping and, 107
  health problems and, 24–25
  home weekend, 231
  life driven by, 9

master, vs planner items, 63–64
number of items on, 134
quick-start program and, 61, 62
PalmPilot and, 117
paper-based planner and, 111–13
Post-it Notes and, 123
WADE Formula for, 62–63
wall or desk calendar and, 108, 109
write it down step and, 63–64
to-dos. *See also* tasks
assessing paper backlog and, 83–84
assigning home or "when" to, 206–8,
  227, 229–31
big-picture goals and, 203
connecting, to big-picture goals, 205–6
delaying, 225–26
goals and activities vs, 199–200
honoring time blocked out for, 238–39
planner as only place for, 104
Post-it planner and, 109, 123
sorting, 201–2, 206–10
SPACE formula and, 200–201
staying ahead of game and, 90–99
in times of crisis, 260
weeding, 86–90
write it down step and, 63–64
toiletries bag, 73
Toshiba Pocket PC e335, 117
toss pile, 88–89
tracking time
common stuck points, 150–51
in daily planner, to improve time
  estimation skills, 47–52
doing math option, 149–50
evaluating log, 151–52
to finding where you spend most,
  145–48
highlight planner option, 148–49
Tracy, Brian, 163
trade-offs, 237
transition periods, 25
travel
making faster, 72–73
time require for, 50, 235
two-page-per-day format, 113–14

unexpected problems, 51
unexpected time, 194
urgency, assigning tasks by, 234–35

variety, 138–39, 235
visual/tactile people, 106–7, 114,
  121–22
voice mail, 26, 253
volunteering, 214–16

WADE Formula, 19, 20, 23, 24, 25,
  61–80
add it up, 62, 64
decide, 62, 64–66
execute your plan, 62, 66–80
write it down, 62–64
waiting, 249, 251
Wall Street Journal, 81
want-tos, converting have-tos into,
  203–5
warranties, 89, 96–97
Web sites, 69, 90, 96–97
weed it down step, for paper, 85–89
week-in-view format, 110, 111
what's holding you back, 17–36
external realities, 18, 24–27
psychological obstacles, 18, 27–36
technical errors, 18, 19–24
three-level diagnostic, 17–19
what's not working, 129–32
what's working, 126–29
wind-down time, 50
wishful thinking, 42
work, 77, 142
big-picture goals and, 159–60
life categories and, 143–44
to-do list, 231
working parents, deleting tasks and,
  211–12, 223–25
workload, 20, 23–24
write it down step, 62, 63–64
defining goals and, 160–61
writing, shortcuts for, 73–75
wrong person for job, 20–21
wrong time for task, 19–20

ABOUT THE AUTHOR

Julie Morgenstern is the founder of Task Masters, a professional organizing company that provides consulting services to individuals and companies like American Express and Sony Music. A columnist for O, *The Oprah Magazine*, she is a frequent guest on TV and radio shows such as *The Oprah Winfrey Show*, the *Today* show, *Good Morning America*, and NPR. Julie lives in New York City with her daughter.

Made in the USA
San Bernardino, CA
22 July 2016